Not All Kids Do Drugs

Lessons in Drug Prevention:
Handbook Four
Proactive Techniques for Teens

By
Miles To Go
Kelly Townsend, Psy.D. & Jonathan Scott

Not All Kids Do Drugs
Lessons in Drug Prevention: Handbook Four
Proactive Techniques for Teens

Order additional copies at www.milestogodrugeducation.com

This book was developed from the Miles To Go Drug Prevention Lecture Series. Miles To Go is based in Southern California.

Thank You to Cathy Belleville of Screen Beans and A Bit Better Corporation for the approved use of their wonderful Screen Beans that brought this book to life!

Additional Clip Art is used with permission from Microsoft Word. For a live link in our e-reader or pdf versions:This way to Microsoft.com

ISBN: **978-1495422133**

Dedication: This book is for every kid who wants to have a full, rich, healthy, safe and exciting life that does not simultaneously give his or her parents heart attacks in the process. As our daughter enters middle school, this book is also for her and her friends—may each of you live without the heartbreak, fear and regret that haunt so many young people as they descend into substance abuse.

Table Of Contents

Introduction

In our work over the past 20 years, Kelly and I have won accolades as the two funniest, best-informed and most influential speakers ever to work for Miles To Go Drug Education. Of course, it helps that we are the only people who have ever worked for Miles To Go, but that's beside the point. Lame jokes aside, though, we really are two of the most popular, well recognized drug educators in California.

For the past two decades, not only have we worked with hundreds of thousands of students in 4th-12th grades, we have also spoken extensively with teachers and parents as well. In addition to our work in schools, we are featured speakers at educational conferences, have videos on the internet, provide opportunities for interns and community service students, and just finished our fourth book, which you are currently reading.

We have not always been prevention specialists. I am a recovering drug addict and alcoholic with over two decades of sobriety; and Kelly, because of her many years working in the entertainment industry, has spent a lifetime surrounded by people like me. If you want all the gory details, you will find our life stories in Part 6.

If you read the dedication, you know that Kelly and I are parents. Our daughter and her friends know Kelly as the fun parent all the kids want to be around, and she works diligently to make sure our house is a safe haven that parents want their kids to come to for fun.

I, on the other hand, am not very socially adept. I can present information well in a classroom or in front of a crowd gathered in the school theater, but comfortable social interactions elude me. Much of my ineptitude is a result of my frequent and ongoing substance abuse as a teen and young adult—I didn't practice sober social interaction then, and so I lack the skill to do it now. It is only one of the many things drugs and alcohol have cost me in my lifetime, but it is our hope that my loss can be your gain. If this book can help you not make the same mistakes I did, then it will have served its purpose.

We want our book to be entertaining and interesting, but there is nothing sadder than adults trying desperately to "write funny" for people decades younger than they are. (Re-read the first two sentences of this section if you need further proof of this point.)

We won't try to write like we're your friends, and our prose won't flow like hip-hop, but we are capable of getting our message across. In the end, it matters, because it is a message that carries life and death consequences for some. We hope you'll give us the benefit of the doubt when it comes to the tone of our writing—it is meant only to be informative and helpful.

Finally, we want to note that this book is for teens and pre-teens, and we will often use the term "kids" to fit this wide range of ages. It is not meant as an insult when we refer to you in that way, and we don't want you to get the impression we are talking down to you.

Jonathan
Summer, 2014

Part 1
Answering The Big Questions

1.1 Why Do Kids Use Drugs?

For every person who has ever made the decision to use drugs or alcohol there exists in that pivotal moment a completely unique set of circumstances: genetics, emotional state, social status, life skills, family, self-image, media influence, stress level, age, friends, and school are only a few of the issues that can contribute to the decision to start using. With that many  elements in play, it seems impossible to identify the real reason why anyone starts using drugs and alcohol.

That said, there is one reason young people cite for doing drugs that comes up repeatedly: stress. Look, it's hard to do well in school, be popular, participate in sports, pursue extracurricular activities, and navigate growing up all while trying to keep your parents happy. Add to that the list of other issues you may struggle with like: romance, bullying, teasing, siblings, physical and mental health problems, divorce issues, step-parents, trouble getting organized, faith, learning disabilities, sex, and on top of all this, you're supposed to get plenty of sleep, which—most of the time—you don't.

 Unfortunately, students who choose to deal with stress by doing drugs fail to understand this basic truth: the very thing they think will reduce the stress in their lives ends up causing even more of

1

it. This can result in a never-ending pattern of stress/use/stress/use that can cause them to spiral out of control very quickly.

In addition, no adequate discussion of drug and alcohol use can be complete without bringing up peer pressure, a subject we feel parents don't fully understand. In fact, we have learned from our students that many of them don't always get it either. Please visit Part 4.2 for a closer look if you want to explain it to your parents or think about it further on your own.

Unfortunately, a large part of the social scene for many teens is parties, and the majority of these parties include the use of drugs and alcohol. For some people, the quickest, easiest, most visible way to fit in at a party is to grab a drink or smoke some weed. A person who lacks a strong, positive self-image will often fall into this trap. It's not just parties where drug and alcohol use starts, either; it can also be the result of boredom, rebellion, curiosity, or the desire to relax and have a good time with friends.

You don't have to be a genius to see that many teens and parents struggle when confronted with the challenge to stay clean, sober and healthy.

Not all is lost, however, for two very important reasons.

1. For almost every factor cited as to why young people ultimately decide to start using drugs, there is a way to redefine what is happening in that instant. That redefining concept is: **drugs are not actually the issue we're dealing**

with—drugs are just a symptom of another problem that isn't being dealt with in a better way.

2. There is always a better solution than drug and alcohol use. That better way is often just simple skills and tools used consistently. No matter what issue you are facing, finding and practicing positive ways to deal with it before reaching for a drink or a drug will not only make you stronger and more skilled in the end, it may save you from a life of abuse or addiction. We will give you as many tools as we can in this book to make sure drug and alcohol use never looks like a good solution to a problem.

Lessons Learned: Why Kids Use

Drug and alcohol use isn't the problem; it's a symptom of an underlying issue that isn't being dealt with effectively. Simple steps, taken consistently when you are young, can prevent you from choosing drugs and alcohol by giving you the skills you need to be effective and comfortable in your life.

1.2 Don't All Kids Eventually Drink Alcohol Or Do Drugs?

It alarms and dismays us how frequently we have to deal with the misconception on the part of many students, parents, teachers, and administrators that all kids will eventually end up drinking or doing drugs before they graduate high school. We cannot emphasize enough how wrong-headed and misinformed this idea is.

The fact of the matter is this: Not All Kids Do Drugs!

We chose it as the title of this book for a reason: because it's true. If you believe what so many people believe—that all kids will eventually use alcohol or drugs—you might be tempted to do so as well in order to fit in with the crowd. Don't! That is a recipe for disaster, and we have to correct this misunderstanding.

Unfortunately, this misperception continues because there always seems to be the parent or teacher who declares, "Let's be realistic—kids are going to drink. There's no way to stop it, so why don't we admit that it's going to happen and do what we can to keep them safe." What they usually mean by "keep them safe" is that drinking teens will be safe as long as they don't drink and drive. Yes, it's true—drunk driving is a stupid, deadly and irresponsible thing to do, but it is a huge mistake to assume that the only danger presented by teen drinking is drunk driving.

Only one in three kids who die after drinking dies in a car crash. Just as many kids who drink and die are actually victims of murder, and kids who drink and die because they commit suicide or overdose on alcohol almost match that number again.

4

We are always tempted to ask the parents who want to keep drinking teens "safe" what plans they have to prevent the murders, suicides and overdoses of those young people. We don't care how many plans parents have in place, they will find themselves panicked and confused as they try to keep a wounded, suicidal or overdosed teen breathing while they wait for the ambulance to arrive.

Our experiences have shown us that the people who insist all kids will use are wrong. We regularly find ourselves talking to parents after one of our presentations who approach us to say something along the lines of:

I've never done a drug in my life

I've never had a drink or smoked a cigarette

 Why, then, do we constantly have to deal with the declarations that all kids are going to drink or do drugs?

There seem to be a number of reasons why:

1. Numerous reports and surveys show that almost all kids end .up using or drinking before they go to college.

Yes, that's true, but it does not mean that most kids drink and do drugs. Ok, you must be starting to think, "Wait a minute! First you say they do, and then you say they don't! Do kids drink and use drugs or not?" Here's what seems to happen: most kids try something once, but only a minority of them continue to use.

→ Yes, almost 8 out of 10 kids will have had at least one drink by 18.

→ But, three out of every four 12th graders don't get drunk on a regular basis.

→ And, less than half of all 12th graders get drunk in their last year of high school. The rest don't—not even once!

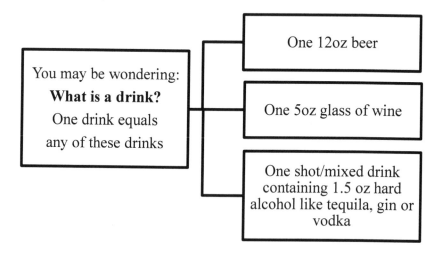

You may be wondering:
What is a drink?
One drink equals
any of these drinks

One 12oz beer

One 5oz glass of wine

One shot/mixed drink containing 1.5 oz hard alcohol like tequila, gin or vodka

And remember, 12th graders use more drugs and alcohol than any other grade. That means the numbers we just looked at are the highest numbers of any grade in high school or middle school.

→ 10th graders use less than 12th graders do, and 8th graders use much less than seniors or sophomores.

→ Remember also: alcohol is the drug students use most often— all the other drugs, including marijuana, are used less frequently than alcohol.

6

So, yes, it looks like lots of kids in high school drink or use drugs, but the fact of the matter is the majority of them <u>do not do so on any regular basis</u>.

When you hear this:

All kids are going to use eventually!

Remember this:

That person has no idea what they are talking about.

2. Another reason some people want to insist that all kids are going to use seems to be that they are trying to make themselves feel better. If that person's child is currently drinking or smoking weed, they are going to feel a lot better about that use if they can convince themselves that it is normal.

Kids who use drugs and alcohol will do the same thing. You will notice this theme as you make your way through high school and college—people who break rules, hurt others, cheat on tests, steal, or act unethically in any way regularly seek to reassure themselves that what they are doing is right, even if they have a huge nagging suspicion that it is actually very wrong.

In fact, we think there are very few kids out there who are currently using drugs or alcohol on a regular basis who don't have some lingering doubt about what they are doing. Please don't ever expect, however, that they will admit this, especially while they are currently engaged in any drug or alcohol use.

We often get to talk with young people who are recovering from drug problems who admit that they knew all along it was a bad idea, they just couldn't say that while they were using. If they voiced doubt about what they were doing, that would have forced them to deal with the idea they were being stupid, and none of us like to feel that way about ourselves.

3. You will also notice, as you make your way through school, that the people who have the most doubt will also be the loudest when it comes to defending their choices. Bullies use violence because they are afraid, and people who doubt their own actions get loud so they can reassure themselves.

Remember this: the louder the voice, the less valid the message. Isn't that weird?

The quiet people are often the ones doing the most important work, and the people who don't use drugs or drink in high school are the ones we never hear from.

Nonusers tend to be scattered among the chess players, the creative writers, the dancers, the musicians, the athletes, the rock climbers, and the actors. Unless they are in a uniquely specialized environment, these different types of kids don't tend to socialize as a group, and they have difficulty identifying and supporting each other. These nonusers need encouragement to continue their conscious choice, and we need to actively encourage healthy alternatives to drug use. If this is to happen, though, we first have to recognize that nonusers even exist, and that will never happen if we keep listening to the claims, "All kids are going to use eventually."

Final thoughts on this section

Of course, it would be foolish for us to think that out of the 10,000 kids we teach each year, not one would drink or get high. We have also heard from some of those who did choose to drink or use drugs. Several of them told us that they stopped before they got into serious trouble; several others went into rehab sooner than they normally would have because of their knowledge that help was available. Many had friends in trouble and were able to help them find their way out of a bad situation.

Unfortunately, there are some students we can no longer hear from; but that we hear of. They are the ones who didn't make it out the other side of the decision to use. They are the ones who died. If you are concerned about drug or alcohol use on the part of a friend, we have included a section on how to help a friend in Part 5.

Lessons Learned: Not All Kids Do Drugs

Don't just look at statistics—look at the real patterns behind them. Not all kids do drugs. In fact, the majority of kids don't use on a regular basis, and many don't use at all. Not using should not be a source of embarrassment. Don't let someone with a big mouth make you doubt the choice to not use. **Remember**: the louder they speak, the more they doubt what they are saying!

9

1.3 Can Kids Use Drugs And Drink Alcohol Safely If A Parent Is Supervising?

If you think back to the previous section, you'll remember the people we spoke of who often declare,

All kids are going to drink—why don't we just have them do it in a safe way?

As we said, one of the ways parents think they can ensure safety on the part of drinking teens is to keep them from driving, and we've already seen where that takes us—and it isn't to safety.

The other concept that constantly crops up in this discussion of "safe teen drinking" is the idea that teens can be safe when they use alcohol if adults supervise them when they drink. This may be one of the more vexing problems we deal with when we discuss alcohol use by teens—so many of the proposed solutions sound incredibly reasonable! If adults just supervise them while they do it, they will be safe! There's just one problem—it doesn't work.

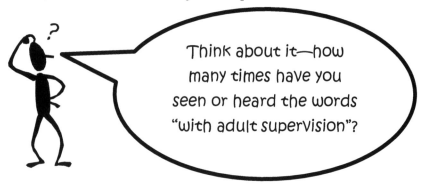

Think about it—how many times have you seen or heard the words "with adult supervision"?

 You can go swimming, but only with adult supervision. You can ride your bike, but only with adult supervision. When you were younger, there was hardly anything in your house you were allowed to touch without adult supervision: knives, scissors, staplers—whatever!

Somehow, we have arrived at the opinion that adult supervision means that things will be safe, and in a perfect world, that would be true. Here's the problem: when it comes to watching kids, some adults have their heads in the clouds.

We're just like you: we space out—a lot!

Usually this isn't the end of the world— the adult is talking on his phone instead of paying attention to the kid with the scissor or knife, and suddenly we're tossing around nicknames like "Nicky Nine Fingers."

Mom is texting her friends while Johnny is trying to figure out what happens when he puts some staples into a DVD (Answer: playability goes WAY down).

Dad starts talking to the neighbor, and the kid on the bike finds herself buried in some hedge—that's just the way it goes.

Unfortunately, the costs of adult lapses in focus can be much worse. Sometimes, kids drown while under adult supervision. Sometimes, cars hit kids while adults are supposed to be watching. One tiny second of inattention can cost a life, and if that's true with something as simple as splashing in a pool or

11

riding a bike, how can adult supervision ever be a safety net when it comes to teen alcohol use?

The answer is, it can't, and the reasons why it can't go beyond the simple fact that adults sometimes have the attention span of a gnat.

As you will see, teen alcohol use is directly associated with future alcohol problems, including abuse and addiction. When adults drink with their kids, those kids end up having more alcohol problems as adults, and that in itself makes it a terrible idea! We will discuss these aspects of the argument against teen drinking in **section 1.6**. Just understand for the moment, though, that teen bodies are built in such a way as to put them at risk when they use alcohol.

Allowing teens to drink under the supervision of adults can result in a variety of complications.

1. Humans are all the same—if you give us an inch, we'll take a mile. When adults give teens permission to drink in their presence, they often don't understand that many teens will translate that into permission to drink whenever they want.

2. Another big problem is the way teens socialize—in big groups. The fact of the matter is when teens drink; they tend to do so most often at parties. Parties, by definition, usually have a whole bunch of people at them.

Adults who imagine they can control teen party drinking are kidding themselves. Even if the adults are totally focused, which is almost impossible, they are going to miss things.

12

Please don't think we are saying that every teen is going to be drinking at every party—we already established in our earlier discussions that most kids don't use regularly.

 However, when teens drink, the ones who do tend to do so in a very unsafe way. In fact, over 90% of teen drinking is what is called "**binge drinking**." Simply put, binge drinking is drinking in such a way as to get drunk quickly.

It is ridiculous to imagine a bunch of teenagers at a party having a quiet discussion as they gently sip from glasses of wine.

That just isn't how it happens,
and adults who imagine it is are in for a shock.

Of the teens who do drink, some will only drink a little, and others will drink A LOT. When people drink too much, the outcomes are predictable: they lose the ability to 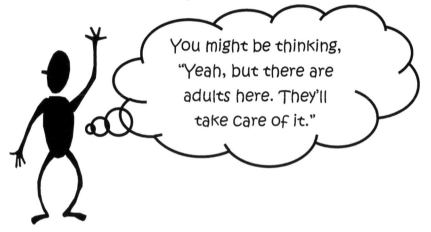 control their behavior, they say outrageous things they don't remember saying, they sometimes get aggressive or violent, the get sick and puke all over the place, and occasionally they lose consciousness or lapse into a coma. Sometimes, they die.

You might be thinking, "Yeah, but there are adults here. They'll take care of it."

Well, they might, but:
1. First, they have to see it happen.
2. Then, they have to know what to do in each individual circumstance.
3. Finally, they have to be willing to do what is required—and there are no guarantees any of this is going to happen.

Supervising teens at parties is like herding cats—you're going to miss a few. If it happens that the adults miss the kid passed out in the corner choking on his own vomit, things can get ugly fast.

14

Most adults can't tell if a drunk kid is asleep, unconscious, or in a coma; and the difference here is critical. Even if the adults do find that kid, they may be reluctant to call an ambulance for him or her.

People in our industry—drug education—know this: an unconscious teen who has been drinking needs medical attention. The problem for the supervising adults is that what they have been allowing to happen is illegal. While it is true that very few adults are ever held accountable for allowing teens to drink under their watch, many of them are not ready to call the police and paramedics when things get dicey.

Adults are just like kids in that way—they don't like to get into trouble. If they can avoid a little discomfort by holding off on the call for the ambulance, many will do so. Unfortunately, that can be a deadly mistake.

Also, as we've already said, another problem with drunk people is that they aren't very smart or very reasonable, and sometimes they get violent. Watching your dad try to wrestle one of your drunken, belligerent friends out of the house is not going to be high on your list of #ThingsIWantToSeeAgain, but you have to realize that it's perfectly possible if your parents let kids drink at your house.

What will you do if one of your friends decides he or she can drive after drinking? Do you or the adults in charge have what it takes to step up and stop them? Trust us, it's harder than it sounds. Drunk people are ridiculously unreasonable and also tend to be dumber than rocks. If you can't talk them out of doing something illogical, we hope you're comfortable with being witness to whatever foolishness they have dreamed up. It might be funny to watch some idiot break his leg in six places on Tosh.O, but it can be pretty sickening to see in reality. We just hope you're ready.

One last thing you have to consider if you're at a party where adults are supervising the use of alcohol by teens: would your parents agree with what is happening?

What would my parents say if they saw me doing this?

You see, this weird thing happens in your mind when you attend a party where the adults in charge are allowing and overseeing the use of alcohol—the adults' presence acts as a form of permission for you to do something you normally wouldn't do. What the heck—if they say it's ok, it must be ok, right?

Some of our students admit attending parties that would freak their parents out if they knew. If some of the nightmare scenarios we've discussed above happen, you should understand that you may end up under the supervision of the police until your parents come to get you.

Are you really looking forward to that moment when you lock eyes with your mom or dad when they come to get you? It's not something teens tend to put a lot of thought into until it's too late.

16

Lessons Learned: Think Before You Party

We hate to be preachy, but you might want to consider some of what we've covered here before you walk into a party where teen drinking or drug use is allowed—and supervised—by adults. Their presence and supervision may give you a sense of security, but the situation you are about to put yourself in is anything but secure.

1.4 What About Kids In Europe? They Drink As Teens, And They Don't Have Any Problems.

We've started to call this one the Zombie Objection—it refuses to die! Americans have developed the idea that Europeans are somehow resistant to the effects brought about by teen alcohol use. It never fails—dozens of times each year a student or parent will insist that teens in other places (but they almost exclusively cite Europe) drink at younger ages and simply don't have the issues with alcohol we have. Once again, what we have here is a case of people saying something is true without any real proof that it is.

What is true:

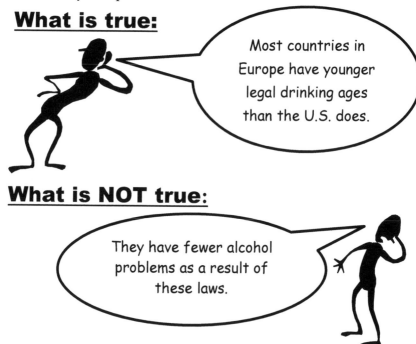

Most countries in Europe have younger legal drinking ages than the U.S. does.

What is NOT true:

They have fewer alcohol problems as a result of these laws.

The argument for using Europe to justify allowing teens to drink really falls apart, though, when you look at the statistics about their actual alcohol use. Not only do Europeans drink more than

18

any other region on earth, their young people have as many or more alcohol problems than the rest of the world does.

These are the facts about European drinking: they drink almost double the amount of alcohol per year compared to the rest of the world. This certainly does not mean that all Europeans are alcoholics, but the inescapable fact of alcohol consumption is that it comes with consequences.

While much of Europe's alcohol use is not the dangerous, heavy binge drinking we've already discussed, their regular heavy use of alcohol makes them more likely to suffer from the more than 40 known alcohol-related illnesses and disorders such as liver disease, alcoholism, and harm to pregnant women and their children.

One out of every seven men in Europe dies from alcohol related causes—we don't think that qualifies as no consequences!

European teens don't fare any better. More European teens have consumed alcohol regularly in the past 30 days than have their American counterparts, and in most European countries, more kids get drunk before the age of 13 than do American teens.

As you will learn in section 1.6, the earlier you drink, the more trouble you have with binge drinking, alcohol abuse, and alcoholism later on. This means that because European teens drink more and earlier than American teens do, they will experience more harm from their drinking than American teens will. In our opinion, this does not qualify as teens drinking and having "no problems," as our questioners constantly insist. In fact, it is the exact opposite.

1.5 Are All Drugs Bad?

We often ask our students what they remember from the previous year's lessons, and (much to our frustration) the most common reply is, "Drugs are bad." While we want to be polite and not shame our students in front of their peers, the urge to scream, "WRONG!" is almost overwhelming. In fact, we make it a point to tell our students there is no such thing as a bad drug. Drugs are objects—the good and bad about them is a result of how people use them. A good drug (one that cures an illness or treats a condition) can turn bad in an instant if you take it incorrectly.

We aren't trying to be purposefully ignorant here. We get it that when people say, "Drugs are bad," they are referring to drugs of abuse—heroin, crystal meth, etc., but it's important to remember that prescription medications and over-the-counter (OTC) medications (such as headache relievers, fever reducers, and cough and cold medications) are drugs as well. If you are suffering because of an illness, they can be extremely beneficial. If you have a condition like asthma or diabetes, medications that treat them can save your life. If you don't have those conditions, though, the medicines used to treat them can kill you as fast as an overdose of heroin will. Drugs aren't good or bad, they are helpful or harmful according to how and when they are taken and who takes them.

Some people make the mistake of thinking that drugs available without a prescription (the OTC's) are risk free. This is simply not true. Some OTC medicines, such as acetaminophen products like Tylenol, have an effective dose that is very close to their dangerous dose, and yet we are amazed how even our older students and many of our parents don't appreciate how dangerous these drugs can be. We constantly remind our students how important it is to read the labels on all medications and follow the dose recommendations to the letter.

Another aspect of prescription and OTC drug abuse is that many young people who abuse them have the mistaken impression that because they come from a doctor, a pharmacy, or a drug store they are "safe." They seem to be missing the fact that "safe" drugs, when abused or misused, immediately become unsafe. Painkillers are literal lifesavers for people with agonizing pain, but they can also cause fatal car accidents, overdoses and addiction when abused by teens who think that, because they are medicine, they are safe.

The ready availability of OTC and prescription drugs has led to a substantial increase in recent teen abuse of these substances. One of the initially unforeseen consequences of prescription drug abuse, though, is that they have the potential to cause dependence and addiction with regular use. When young people abusing these drugs discover that they are hard to get regularly, they often resort to the use of street drugs. This is one of the major causes of the recent upswing in heroin use in the U.S.—people who start out abusing pharmaceutical opiates like Vicodin and OxyContin end up using street heroin in the end because it's cheaper and more readily available.

Over the past decade, we have also seen a significant increase in the abuse of ADHD drugs. Because these drugs are stimulants, students think they can increase the amount of studying and schoolwork they do by taking them. Unfortunately, the cost ends up being excessively high for the supposed benefits they gain. Not only do students who abuse ADHD drugs run the risk of addiction and overdose, not one study has shown any measurable increase in learning or intelligence because of this use.

While students with ADD/ADHD can benefit greatly from the use of these drugs, those without the condition are treading on dangerous ground when they seek improved performance in the so-called "study drugs." If you need more energy to study, the only place you will ultimately find long-term gain is in a healthy diet, regular exercise, and adequate sleep.

We are completely aware of how that sounds: BOOOOOORRRRIIINNNNG! But this is part of what growing up means—getting a job done without resorting to cheating or tricks.

One drug almost nobody thinks of when discussing OTC's is **caffeine**. The world consumes a staggering amount of caffeine, and while it isn't recognized as dangerous when consumed in moderate doses by adults, very little information suggests that teens should be using it regularly. Unfortunately, caffeine is a big money maker these days, and teen use represents a big segment of that bonanza. Energy drinks cost pennies to make and yet they sell for dollars per dose, and these extreme profit margins allow the companies selling energy drinks to spend tons of cash on marketing.

Energy drinks are just like many other products, though—there is very little difference from one type to the next. When this happens, companies don't try to sell you the product anymore, but instead sell you a lifestyle. Take a quick look at the majority of energy drink ads. What are they telling you? You'll be led to think that if you drink Energy Drink A, you'll suddenly be in a band—and you're the lead guitarist! If, instead, you drink Energy Drink B, you'll magically transform into a world class snowboarder. Gold medal, here I come!

Here's the problem—caffeine is still just caffeine.

Dose for dose, the coffee brewed at your local coffeehouse has more of it than the average energy drink does. The bigger problem, though, is that both the coffee and the energy drink have big doses of caffeine—more than young people have ever consumed before. Caffeine does not have magical powers to transform you into a Marvel character, but it does have the power to mess you up if you use too much of it or use it too often.

So, what are you supposed to do?

Nutrition Facts:	
Caffeine	???
Splat	75mg
Junk	50mg
Sugar	99mg
Crud	82mg
Salt	98mg
Stuff we can't pronounce	400mg

The same thing you do with other OTC's: read the label! The trouble with caffeine products is that they frequently don't have the information you need listed anywhere on the container. You may have to do some homework in order to find the information, and that's a ridiculous suggestion in most cases. If you're in line to order your favorite coffee drink, there's very little chance you'll take the time to look up the caffeine content of said beverage. In this case, you'll have to do the work ahead of time.

First: find out how much caffeine you can safely consume.

Here's the answer: none.

For some of you, though, that's just not going to cut it. Some of you are going to insist on consuming caffeine, so we'll give you another recommendation we've seen suggested as a relatively safe dose for teens:

One milligram (mg) of caffeine per day for each kilogram (kg) of body weight.

What are most of you going to get from that suggestion? Nothing.

So here's an example of what that means:

100
LBS=
45kg

If a teen weighs 100 pounds, that's about 45kg.
In theory, then, that person could safely consume
45mg of caffeine per day.

How much is that?

→ About 16oz. of cola,

→ just over 4oz. of the average energy drink,

→ or 2-3oz. of coffee from your favorite Seattle coffee brewer.
As you can see, if you are using caffeine at all, you are probably
using way more than many doctors and researchers say you
should be using.

Do yourself a favor—don't establish a caffeine habit when
you're young. If you're relying on caffeine to get the job done,
you're in a dependent situation, and it will only get worse as you
get older.

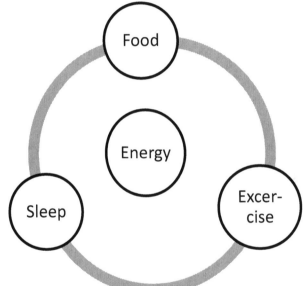

You'll ultimately discover that the truth is still the truth—you're
going to get energy from good food, moderate exercise, and the
right amount of sleep.

✓ There are no shortcuts,

✓ There are no cheats.

✓ Get used to it.

Lessons Learned:
Here Are Some Suggestions For Taking OTC's
And Prescription Drugs

→ Never take any medicine or drug unless your parents know about it and have given you permission to use it.

→ Check for expiration dates. This includes commonly used medications like Tylenol, Advil, Aleve, etc. If you take expired medicine, it might not work as well as it should, which could lead to more frequent or larger doses than are safe. Some medicines, such as tetracycline, become toxic after their expiration date.

→ Read the label and follow the directions. At a minimum, you should read all sections that have anything to do with dose, safety, warnings, dangers, and especially a section called "contraindications," which warns you about other drugs, foods, and beverages that should not be consumed at the same time as the medicine.

→ NEVER share medications. Don't take medicine intended for others; don't give your medicine to others. Not only is it unsafe, it's illegal.

1.6 What Are The Warning Signs Of Addiction?

One of the unavoidable facets of discussions about alcohol and drug abuse is that they tend to highlight the worst possible outcomes: addiction and alcoholism. We are not saying that everyone who uses drugs or alcohol will ultimately end up addicted to them. That simply isn't true.

What is true, though, is some people do up end as addicts and alcoholics. In the past, we couldn't really tell who it was going to happen to. While we still don't have a crystal ball of addiction and alcoholism, we can predict an increase in the chance it will happen to you if you have what are called **"risk factors."**

If you currently have or will have in the future any of these risk factors, the chances that you will become an addict or alcoholic are much greater.

 If you have more than one, the possibility of addiction increases dramatically. Unfortunately, very few people know what these factors are. You, however, are going to be different. When you are done reading this section, you'll know more than most of the population does about how to assess your risks.

In the following section, we're going to outline five of the major risk factors that make you more likely to experience addiction or alcoholism in your lifetime. We'll end the section with a list of other things associated with a higher likelihood of addiction to keep in mind as well. For now, though, the five risk factors:

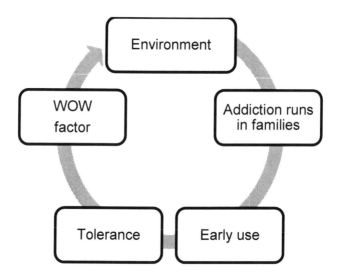

1. ENVIRONMENT

This first risk factor is actually not directly associated with addiction, but you've probably already figured out that in order to become addicted to something, you first have to use it—uh, duh. A big environmental risk factor for starting the use of drugs or alcohol is spending time in the presence of people who use them.

This will typically not be a case of one of your friends constantly badgering you to get drunk or high, although that may happen occasionally. (We will devote an entire section of this book, section 4.2, to a detailed discussion of peer pressure.) This, however, is usually a much more subtle effect.

Here's why regular exposure matters: humans get used to stuff really fast. Strange things become normal, bad smells become unnoticeable, repetitive noises eventually melt into the background, and most importantly for our discussion, drugs and alcohol lose the ability to shock us after a while.

 The first time you see your friends drink, it will probably freak you out. The tenth time, not so much. Eventually, you're going to get used to having drugs and alcohol around you—you will come to accept them as normal. **That's not good.**

Another thing will also start to happen as you spend time around users—you're going to be curious about what it is they are experiencing when they use. Drunk

29

people often act really silly, and silly often looks like fun. People who smoke marijuana often find the dumbest stuff funny. If your friend spends twenty minutes laughing at the way a certain word sounds, you're going to wonder what the heck is so funny. Eventually, you may want to see for yourself, and you'll end up experimenting to find out. Unfortunately, you just started using. Bad news for you.

The big problem you'll face as you spend more and more time around people who use is you're going to notice that drugs and alcohol have the power to make them not feel things for a while. Unfortunately, life happens to be kind of cruel on occasion. At some point, you are going to find yourself with a broken heart or a bruised ego, and all of a sudden, that drug or that drink might start to look attractive.

People don't like pain. We try to avoid it, and if we have it, we want to get rid of it. If a drink or drug promises you relief from an unpleasant feeling, it will start to look pretty appealing, especially if you are really hurting.

At first, it might seem like a good thing that the bad feelings will be less intense for a while. Unfortunately for you, the effects of what you took will start to wear off, and guess what happens to those feelings that went away for a while? They come back, and they haven't lost any of their power. You're also going to notice something else, as well—you feel a little crappy as a result of having used alcohol or drugs, and that pain gets added to the old garbage you were already dealing with.

30

You can probably see where this is going, can't you?

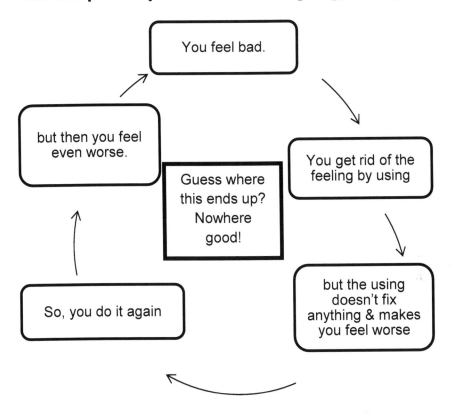

How do you avoid all this confusion and temptation?

Don't spend time around people who drink and use drugs. If you never do them, drugs and alcohol can never have any power to cause you to become an addict or alcoholic. When you choose to surround yourself with positive, non-using, non-drinking peers, you will automatically reduce the risk of seeking solace or acceptance via the path of drug and alcohol use. It's that simple.

2. ADDICTION RUNS IN FAMILIES

One of the major things we have learned about addiction is that it is influenced very powerfully by genetics. If your parents have curly hair, you probably do too. If they have freckles, you probably do too. Unfortunately, if one of your parents ever was, is, or ever will be a drug addict or alcoholic, you have a much greater risk of becoming one also. Bummer.

This is not a small risk—the numbers here are daunting. Parental addiction and alcoholism increases the risk for their offspring by as much as four times!

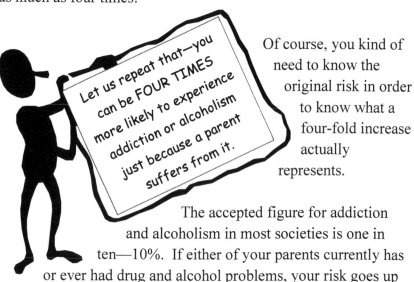

Let us repeat that—you can be FOUR TIMES more likely to experience addiction or alcoholism just because a parent suffers from it.

Of course, you kind of need to know the original risk in order to know what a four-fold increase actually represents.

The accepted figure for addiction and alcoholism in most societies is one in ten—10%. If either of your parents currently has or ever had drug and alcohol problems, your risk goes up to 40% or more--ALMOST HALF!

It gets even worse if both your parents experienced or currently have problems with drugs or alcohol. Some indications show that kids with two addict or alcoholic parents can exhibit addiction rates of 60%!

So where does that leave you?

First, you have to work with accurate information. Most parents don't want their kids to think poorly of them, and that can lead them to keeping secrets in an effort to avoid disappointment on the part of their kids. If you're old enough to be reading this book, though, you need to know—you deserve to know—if the people in your family tree have drug or alcohol issues.

So ask them!

Please don't think this information is all bad. Nobody wants a loved one to suffer from any disease, but if you find out that your family history puts you at risk for drug and alcohol addiction, that can be the thing that gives you the strength to say, **"No thanks, I'm good"** when a friend or fellow party-goer offers you a drink or a drug. If you end up not drinking or using drugs because of problems your parents had, that's fantastic!

No thanks, I'm good.

We may not have the power to change the past, but we can use it to create a much better future.

Seeking this knowledge can be uncomfortable for everyone involved. Some parents may think that questions like these indicate that you are planning to drink and do drugs. Don't let that stop you. You can remove some of that fear by reassuring your parents that this is an exercise in information, not a plan for abuse.

33

You might say something like:

You know, I don't really see myself drinking or doing drugs, but I read something today that made me think. It said that adults troubled by addiction and alcoholism could pass those problems on to their kids. It made me wonder if I might be one of those kids. Am I?

You may think:

Why the heck would I have to ask? If my parents had drug or alcohol problems, I'd obviously know it!

34

Not true. Maybe their problematic drug or alcohol use happened years ago—before you were even born.

It still has the power to put you at risk!

→ They don't pass the potential for addiction on to you because of their use, they pass it on because they themselves were born with a genetic predisposition to drug and alcohol problems.

→ You don't inherit the problematic use, you inherit the genetic predisposition for problematic use.

Here's what else you have to consider: many people who suffer from addiction and alcoholism get REALLY good at hiding it. Sometimes addiction and alcoholism can go on for years, even decades, before anyone finds out.

One of the first things we teach our students in our introduction class is that drug addiction and alcoholism are invisible to the untrained eye. That does **not** mean your normal looking parents are actually addicts and alcoholics! It just means you can't assume that appearances always reflect reality, so you have to ask the questions. It's the only way you'll get the most accurate information possible.

One last thing about addiction running in families: your parents aren't the only ones who can pass problems on to you. Even if both your parents never had, don't have, or ever will have addiction or alcoholism, you may still inherit some risk from your grandparents. While that risk is less powerful than if it came straight from you parents, it is not meaningless. We don't want to spoil your memories of Granny and Grandpa, but part of growing up consists of taking the good with the bad.

Remember, problems with drugs and alcohol don't make people bad, or weak, or any other negative thing you can think up. It just means that these people are built in such a way that drug and alcohol use hurts them more than it does others. Ultimately, though, if there are any issues with your grandparents, you need to know.

3. EARLY USE

If you start drinking or using drugs at a young age, you directly increase your chances of alcoholism and addiction.

> ## Because this risk factor is so big, we're going to repeat that:
>
> If you start drinking or using drugs as a pre-teen or young teen, you will have drug and alcohol problems that are dramatically larger than if you wait until you are 21 or older to start anything.

How big is the risk?

If a 14-year-old drinks regularly (gets drunk six times each month) he will be an alcoholic at a rate of 47% as an adult!

 Think about that—one out of every two 14-year-olds who drink regularly will be an alcoholic as an adult, and this is before you add in any other risk factors!

In the cases where more than one risk factor is present, the numbers get big fast. Some reports say that if you drink regularly at 14 **and** have a family history of addiction or alcoholism, you will be an addict or alcoholic at a rate of up to 90%.

Yes, you read that right—**9 in ten people** with risk factor two (addiction runs in families) and three (early use) combined will be in trouble with drugs or alcohol in their adult lives.

37

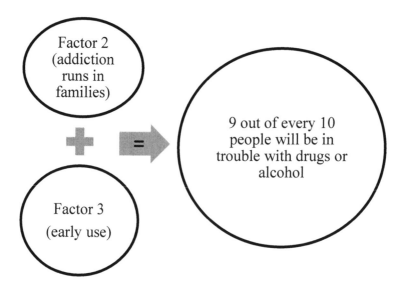

Factor 2 (addiction runs in families)

+

=

Factor 3 (early use)

9 out of every 10 people will be in trouble with drugs or alcohol

That is beyond scary—it's devastating.

This risk doesn't just exist with alcohol, either—it exists with **all the drugs** teens are most likely to use. For instance, a teen who starts smoking marijuana at the age of 17 or younger is two to three times more likely to be addicted to it than he or she would be than if the use started in adulthood. By the way, that doesn't mean we want you to smoke weed as an adult, either! It just means it hurts teens more.

Think About This: one out of every four teenagers smoking marijuana today is going to suffer dependence and addiction problems with the drug. And remember, this is a drug that a lot of people (especially teens) insist isn't even addictive.

It goes on—teens who smoke tobacco are much more likely to get addicted to it, and their addictions are more powerful and longer lasting than people who start smoking later on.

→ You get the point—if you start using drugs or alcohol as a teen, you will have much higher rates of addiction and alcoholism as an adult.

When you hear this:

Remember this:

When you see how high the risk of addiction is for teen users, you probably wonder...

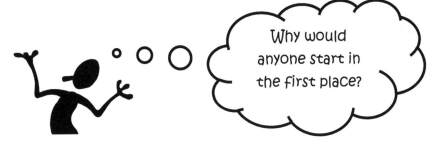

How can they ignore such obvious dangers?
There are a couple of reasons.

Nobody thinks it will happen to him or her. This is just human nature. If you tell a person that something they are doing has the power to cause them harm, they usually respond by telling you that, while they understand it hurts some people, it won't hurt them because….and then they list the reasons:

I'm too smart,

I'm too tall,

I'm too strong,

I'm too pretty,

I'm too handsome, etc.

It's kind of amazing what high opinions people have of themselves!

The problem, though, is that drug addiction and alcoholism don't care about those things. Tall people get addicted the same way the vertically challenged do.

40

Here's the way risk factors work most of the time—if you expose yourself to them, you will suffer the consequences even if other factors are present. That means your beauty won't stop you from becoming an alcoholic one out of every two times if you insist on drinking regularly at the age of 14.

That's just the way it is.

Add to this the fact that teens who use rarely look like anything bad is happening to them. Sure, kids who drink too much may end up feeling really sick the next day (the classic hangover), or they may do something really stupid or embarrassing that they later regret, but after the alcohol wears off they can usually still walk and talk and do homework the same way they could before getting drunk.

This outward appearance of being ok, though, is masking the reality of what's actually happening on the inside. It has only been within the past few years that we have gained the ability to observe what happens to human brains when they are exposed to drugs and alcohol, and the evidence shows that teen brains are directly changed and damaged by drug and alcohol use.

Ok, so we can now show that drinking and drug use by teens is bad for them, but rarely do we have any immediate evidence that proves what we are saying.

The sad fact is that the addictions associated with teen drug and alcohol use often don't show up for years, sometimes even decades, after the use begins.

This leaves us with a big problem. Unless we can show

41

kids direct, measurable harm that is caused by their use, they often don't believe anything bad is happening. Sometimes, they will directly ignore or deny changes that everyone around them can clearly see.

Ultimately, we just have to keep trying. This is relatively new information we are sharing with you, and not many people know as much as you now do about the effects of teen drug and alcohol use on future addictions.

All we really hope for right now is that you will respect the power of this risk factor and choose to avoid the use of drugs and alcohol. If you can do that, you will be saving yourself and your loved ones the potential of limitless heartbreak and sorrow. That's some pretty powerful stuff.

4. TOLERANCE YOU ARE BORN WITH

When people drink too much alcohol, they get drunk. When they do drugs, they get high. Aren't you glad you read this book? Now you know things NOBODY ELSE KNOWS!

Actually, just about everybody knows these things. What very few people know, though, is that there are wide variations in the ways people experience drugs and alcohol, and one reason this happens is genetic factors they were born with.

It's generally true that people who drink more alcohol get drunker than people who drink less. Some people, though, can drink much larger amounts before they start to feel alcohol's effects. This is not a case of one person being physically larger than the other, which would also change how a certain number of drinks affected each of them. This, instead, is a matter of genetics—some people are born with a much higher resistance to alcohol's effects.

This resistance to alcohol can be misleading. Many people we talk to believe that if you don't get drunk when you drink, chances are low that you will become an alcoholic. The thinking goes, "If you don't feel anything, how would you ever get addicted?" On the surface, that makes sense, but the truth is much different.

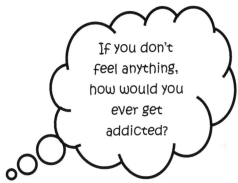

Picture a scene where two people are drinking together. The first person has a normal response to the alcohol, and starts to exhibit signs of drunkenness like laughing loudly, acting in ways they normally wouldn't (you know—swinging from chandeliers, telling dirty jokes to a priest—classic old movie stuff), and generally acting like a monkey. Person number two, on the other hand, doesn't feel any difference at all.

The second person is left with two choices:
1) Give up, and just accept that alcohol has no effect, or 2) keep drinking until they do feel something. Unfortunately, most people choose option 2, and this is where the problems start.

Evidence has shown over the years that people with a high resistance to alcohol not only drink in much greater quantity than normal, they also drink much more frequently than others do. Both of these factors increase the likelihood they will eventually end up as alcoholics.

It's important to note that this risk factor is less powerful than the first three, but you still need to consider its effects, especially if other factors are also present.

5. THE "WOW!" FACTOR

Almost every single person who ends up addicted to drugs or alcohol can tell you a story about the day his or her life changed, and that change often resulted from the perceived effects drugs or alcohol had. Addicts and alcoholics often report that they had a profoundly powerful reaction to the drug that ultimately enslaved them. The experience for many is so powerful that this risk factor has earned the nickname The "Oh my God!" Moment.

The reasons for this reaction aren't clearly understood, but many researchers think that there may be a problem with the way addicts experience pleasure. One of the things that surprise people when they first start learning about drugs is that substances that can cause addiction and alcoholism activate a system in the human brain that usually deals with pleasure and reward.

We will talk about this in detail in part 4.1, but for now you need to know that humans have developed so that activities that ensure survival are rewarded by a pleasure-causing chemical in the brain called dopamine. Some people (addicts and alcoholics, in this case) have a lowered response to pleasurable activities—either they don't have enough dopamine in parts of their brains or they react to the dopamine that is present in a less intense way.

Because of this lack, when they do come upon a situation where dopamine is present in large amounts—in other words, when they drink or do drugs—they have an experience that is profoundly powerful.

The unlucky souls who discover that this is true for them are stuck in a terrible place—they have found a powerful, reliable way to feel really good, but that good feeling requires that they use drugs or alcohol to achieve it.

It would be tempting to think,

No problem. Every once in a while, they just use the thing that makes them feel good, and then they can go back to living their normal lives.

The problem gets more obvious when you learn that human brains have another behavior that's very predictable: when they feel pleasure, they want to feel it again and again. It seems like the brain's

45

motto is, "If a little is good, more is great—and the sooner, the better." So, if a person feels an immense sense of well-being or pleasure when he or she does drugs, they will immediately get a message from their brain telling them to do it again and again. It doesn't take a genius to see where this is headed.

One of the more unfortunate aspects of this risk factor (also true for #4: tolerance) is that you can only tell if you have it by using a drug or alcohol and then discovering its presence in you. While we're big advocates for self-knowledge, this is an experiment better left undone. Rather than trying to figure out if you have the last two risk factors through experience, we would rather you just appreciate how bad the news will be if you find the answer is yes. It's better just to avoid the whole mess by not starting to use in the first place.

While the five risk factors listed above have the power to predict higher rates of use and addiction in large groups, they still can't tell any individual whether he or she will become an addict or alcoholic. Please understand, though, that the more risk factors you exhibit, the higher the chances are that any use on your part will turn out badly.

You should also understand that these aren't the only factors to consider as you assess your current risk status.

46

Other things you should keep in mind include:

STRESS -- Young people who perceive themselves to be under great stress have higher use rates than teens who are less overwhelmed. Try to find some other way to deal with stress, though, because the truth about drugs and alcohol is that they actually result in more stress, not less.

RISK TAKING AND POOR IMPULSE CONTROL -- Kids who seek abnormally high levels of stimulation and those who have trouble saying no to temptation both show increased levels of drug and alcohol use. Are you an adrenaline junkie? Do you have trouble saying no to risk? Better you put on a helmet and some knee and elbow pads and take up an extreme sport than start using drugs and alcohol. The former might hurt you, the latter definitely will.

TROUBLE IN SCHOOL --Not doing well in school is powerfully linked with drug and alcohol use. If you have poor grades or struggle in other ways (skip school, defy teachers and administrators, or lack the drive to do well) you are more likely to abuse substances. Try to find a mentor or role model who can help you figure out why school isn't ringing your bell, so to speak.

LITTLE OR NO PARENTAL OVERSIGHT -- Kids who lack parental oversight are more likely to abuse drugs and alcohol. You may not want your parents all up in your business, but imagine what it would be like if they didn't care if you lived or died. Some kids actually have that problem, and they are the first to tell us that they would love it if someone actually cared enough to ask them where they are going or who they are going to be hanging out with.

47

As you read over the risk factors listed above, please remember that having one or more of them present in your life does **NOT** mean that you are definitely going to be an addict or alcoholic.

It **DOES** mean that you are at increased risk if you start using substances, especially if you start early. You can completely remove the power of risk factors to predict your future by avoiding use altogether. We know—easier said than done, but well worth the effort in the end! Please consider the option of not using.

Lessons Learned: The Five Warnings

If you exhibit any of the five risk factors for addiction, understand that they don't predict individual outcomes. They do predict increased risk. Learn what you need to in order to assess your risk profile as accurately as possible. Ask questions, contemplate how your life is going, then change what you can. Avoid situations or people with the power to awaken a risk factor you can't control.

Part 2
How To Survive Your Teen Years

2.1 The Big Three

We want you to do an exercise with us. Whoa! Did you see that? The first sentence in a new section and half of you already hate what's going on! Just to be clear: Jonathan also hates it when a presenter says something like, "Ok, we're going to do an exercise. Everybody stand up and face the person next to you!" His immediate reaction is to check for the nearest exits. Jonathan. Hates. Exercises. Now that we've cleared that up, we still beg you to indulge us—please do the exercise.

What we want you to do is think back to the most enjoyable thing you ever did with your parents. We understand that in today's world, that can be a confusing request—so many families have parent structures that don't just consist of the original Mom/Dad pairing (heck, at one point our daughter had like five grandfathers), so if you have a different situation, think about your favorite memory of the parent you are currently living and dealing with.

One of the most common features of almost every favorite parent memory will be one of closeness, of bonding, of that special understanding only a parent and child can have. The setting probably won't be the central part of your memory—it could be Angel Stadium, or Half Dome at Yosemite, or the beach, or a movie theater or dance floor—it really isn't as important as the feelings you had in that moment.

49

Now that you have your favorite memory, we want you to do one more thing—ask yourself if you are still close with your parents. Do you talk easily at the dinner table each night? Do car trips pass almost without notice because your conversations with your parents are so engaging? If the answer is yes, that's so cool. If it isn't yes, then your memory just turned a little sad, didn't it?

The bond between parent and child is the closest one you will ever have—if it is whole. Unfortunately, that bond can be seriously  tested, even broken, during your teen years. This section is designed to help you maintain a close bond with your parents during this potentially rocky time. If your default setting is dull, sullen, ear bud-inspired silence when you are with your parents, it's time to change that. While your parents may not currently be your best friends, they don't have to be total strangers either. It's just that we think the close, communicative thing is much better.

Another thing this section will do is help you avoid the use of drugs and alcohol. We contend that it is almost impossible for you to have a close relationship with your parents while you are drinking or using drugs. The only way you could be drinking or using without having to deceive your parents would be if they were allowing it or doing it with you, and that's just ridiculously unhealthy and unsafe.

Here are a few suggestions that will help you continue or establish and maintain a healthy, close relationship with your parents during middle and high school.

We call them The Big Three:
1. Let your parents play an active role in your teenage life.
2. Have and observe a curfew.
3. Have a stated family policy of non-use on the part of the kids.

Let's look at each of those in a little more detail:

1. **Let your parents have an active role in your teenage life.** One of the most important tasks you are supposed to accomplish as a young adult is to become your own person and separate from your parents. That doesn't mean, however, that you end your relationship with them. It is possible (and healthy) to become an individual while still maintaining close relationships with family and friends, and part of that is allowing your parents to have an active role in your life. There are a number of things you can do to accomplish that:

Let your parents know what's happening at school. We are not talking about having them micromanage your homework question by question, but let them know what's going on with the big stuff.

✓ When is the midterm?
✓ When is the science fair?
✓ When is the play?
✓ When is the game?

When something big happens, tell them how it went. Your parents appreciate how busy you are, but they really want to be a part of your life. Talking to them about your school day helps them to do that.

Introduce your friends to your parents. We know how important your friends are to you. A good friend can change your life, but a bad one can permanently alter or end it. Most of your friends are probably great, but everyone can be fooled occasionally. Having your parents as a second set of eyes can help you identify a friendship that might not be as positive as it seems on the surface. Understand that your parents have a lot more

experience than you do when it comes to identifying toxic people and relationships. This doesn't mean your parents should judge your friends solely on their clothes or their hair, but it does mean that if a particular friend is leading you into questionable emotional, physical, or ethical areas, your parents might be able to help you see that.

Just so you know—if your friends are drinking or doing drugs they are a direct threat to your immediate and future health and safety. Don't expect your parents to support such a relationship. You also have to realize that if you are hanging out with a bunch of drinkers and drug users it will be next to impossible to have a healthy, communicative relationship with your parents. Is that really a price you want to pay? If it is, we suggest you might want to spend some time analyzing the path you find yourself on.

Understand peer pressure. Peer pressure may be one of the more loaded and misunderstood concepts we deal with. Most adults we meet think there is some monstrous group of adolescents out there actively and aggressively trying to force their children to change and conform. Many young people we meet say they see the term peer pressure, when used by adults, as a two-pronged insult—your friends are out to hurt you and you are bound, like some sort of brain-damaged sheep, to mimic any behavior you witness. This does not mean peer pressure isn't massively powerful, we just think it's much more subtle than the way many parents see it. For a complete overview, please see section 4.2.

Meet your friends' parents, and introduce them to your parents. No, you don't have to have close relationships with the parents of every casual acquaintance in your life, but if you are going to be spending significant amounts of time with some of your friends, your parents and theirs should know each other.

You should be willing to discuss your media choices with your parents. We understand this one is difficult—the video games you most want to play are often the exact same ones your parents have forbidden you even to look at. This goes beyond video game violence and sex, though. For example, the number of smoking scenes you witness in movies and on television is directly related to the likelihood you will smoke. You can lessen this effect, though, if you analyze and talk about smoking scenes after the show or movie is over, and your parents are often one of the best resources you have for this kind of discussion.

Also, while it can sometimes lead to some really embarrassing and clueless posts, you should include your parents in your social media profile—Facebook, Instagram, and the ten other online entities that will have become popular in the time between this sentence being written and the actual publication. Hey, two months is an eternity in social media adoption and dismissal cycles! See more about your parents and your media in section 2.6, the Internet.

Make sure that your parents know your teachers and coaches. While this may seem obvious to you, it might not be to your parents. Make sure they know who is who and what your relationship is with each person.

Eat dinner with your family as often as you can. The Center for Addiction and Substance Abuse (CASA) at Columbia University, in a study sponsored by Nickelodeon, showed that one of the most positive things you can do is eat dinner with your family. Dinners didn't prove to be magical, but they do play a big role in maintaining the relationships that foster healthy communication in families. Take half an hour to enjoy dinner with your family—you have to eat anyway, so just consider this an exercise in multi-tasking.

2. **Have and observe a curfew.** Let's face it—nobody likes having a curfew. When your parents tell you to be home by a certain time, it feels like you are being controlled, and nobody likes that either. So why do we recommend that you have one? Seriously—you didn't just ask that, did you?

First, without a curfew, some kids would only go home to eat and do laundry. Second, and more realistically, spending a lot of unsupervised free time with your friends, especially late at night, can lead to a host of troubles. Young people who hang around with other unsupervised teens are more likely to have problems with drug use, sexual activity, and other undesirable behaviors and emotional difficulties.

Curfews are not just fixed points in time, though. The goal of a curfew is to make sure that you are where you're supposed to be, and when you're done, you come home. The best curfews are reasonable and take into account how long it will take you to travel to, experience, and return from whatever supervised activity you are attending.

If the movie ends at 8:30, dinner takes an hour, and travel time to get to the restaurant and then home afterward is 45 minutes, your curfew should be around 10:15.

Unfortunately, some parents seem to just grab an arbitrary point out of thin air and act like it is the sacred time of return. When this is the case, their kids can end up missing many safe, sane experiences with their friends simply because they exceed the arbitrary curfew by a few minutes. When it comes to curfews, parents should note that a little flexibility can go a long way.

You, on the other hand, have to understand that there is a general rule of thumb in play here: the later you are out, the greater the chances you are going to get into trouble. When we speak of flexibility, we do not mean you should be able to hang out with your friends until the wee hours of the morning just because you want to.

To us, there aren't many valid reasons you would be out socially on a school night, and although older kids can be out later than younger ones can, there isn't any reason for them to be out on a weekend night after midnight at all. (Please note: if you are a middle school student reading this, we did not just recommend a curfew of midnight for you. You knew before you even read this that wasn't what we meant. Midnight is for seniors in high school. You—not so much.)

Think about it this way: curfews, like consequences, are your friends. They serve to keep you out of situations where you are spending large blocks of time unsupervised with large groups of your friends. Certainly, not every large teen social gathering ends up in disaster, but a few do, and curfews lessen that number substantially.

55

3. **Have a Stated Policy of Non-Use.** We have occasionally sent surveys home with our students. The students are supposed to interview their parents and fill in the answers themselves. We were surprised by some of the answers we got to the question, "Do you have a stated policy of non-use for the children in your family?" Frequently, the handwriting on the answer sheets changed for that particular answer—the adults had apparently taken the answer sheets from the children and started answering in their own handwriting. Often, the answers started with words to the effect, "It should go without saying that drug use is not allowed in this house!" We want this to be clear: If it goes without saying, it goes unsaid.

Parents who assume their kids understand that drug use is undesirable are missing an important point—if parents don't say it, kids don't know it. In fact, parents who regularly and clearly state that drug and alcohol use is off limits cut the chances their children will do either by massive amounts. Some studies show that alcohol and marijuana use can be cut by five to seven times when parents take this simple step, so when your parents start in on the same old thing about not drinking or doing drugs, just nod your head and know they love you.

Unfortunately, parents often wait too long to have conversations with their kids about drugs. Many seem to think that their kids won't think about drugs if they just don't mention them—they hope the subject never comes up.

Actually, the earlier families start these conversations about curfews, expectations and values, the more opportunities they will have to continue the conversation. Numerous studies show that one of the major reasons teenagers cite for not using drugs is that they don't want to disappoint or embarrass their parents.

If your parents haven't laid out a clear set of expectations, don't be afraid to show them this section and ask them, "Hey, uh, what's our family policy on drug and alcohol use, er, I mean non-use?" We always tell parents, "If you let your kids know exactly what you want, they may surprise you—they may do everything they can to meet your expectations!"

Think About This: Do You Know The "Cool" Parent?
Parents who try to win the favor of their children by being the "cool" parent are completely missing the point, in our opinion. Years ago, Jonathan was having lunch with a group of juniors when one young man said of another, "His mom is really cool. She lets us drink beer and smoke weed with her." In an absolute deadpan, the other young man said, "I have plenty of friends. What I wish I had was a real mom."

Remember, if your parents don't parent you, there is often nobody else to fill that spot. They don't have to be mean and unfriendly, but they do have to do their job. As you grow into adulthood, the respect they earn by parenting you well will pay the dividend of a lifetime of friendship.

Lessons Learned:
Start With These Three Simple Things
If you let your parents have an active role in your life, set and observe curfews, and have a stated family policy of non-use on your part, you will have laid down a foundation that will allow you and your family to experience a healthy, life-long relationship based on love and mutual respect.

2.2 What On Earth Is A Family Mission Statement, And Why Would I Want To Create One With My Family?

If there were ever to be a contest that awarded prizes for "words most likely to make teens run away screaming in terror," the phrase "family mission statement" would be way up there in the rankings. We think even most adults regard family mission statements the same way they would view working on tax returns and cleaning litter boxes. With that in mind, you may be wondering why we recommend them and, more to the point, what the heck they even are! Well, we recommend them because they really can make a difference, not only in your ability to resist offers of drugs and alcohol but also in how closely your actions match your beliefs.

As for the definition of mission statements: when people think about them, they usually picture corporate declarations of what a business stands for and what it hopes to accomplish. Jonathan recently bought a pair of shoes from the online retailer Zappos, and was impressed by the clarity and brevity of their corporate mission statement, "To provide the best customer service possible."

Unfortunately, many companies forget the short and sweet philosophy and publish mission statements that could put The Energizer Bunny into a coma. That, obviously, is not what we are going for here.

Family mission statements have to fall somewhere in between these two extremes. For example, it would be nice simply to say, "To provide the best family experience possible," but trying to figure out what that means is nearly *imp*ossible! You have to add a little more detail than that if anyone is to benefit from your family's statement. Of course, you'll probably want to include some core beliefs most families would agree are good, like honesty and respect, but after that you can go just about anywhere in declaring who you are as a family. We hope that your family's mission will be very personal and unique as it outlines your goals, dreams, and beliefs.

Our mission:
To provide the best family experience possible

Developing this mission statement is like creating a scrapbook, but before the events happen. Instead of pasting together images of things in the past, you make a list of all the things you believe in and want to have happen, thereby creating a scrapbook of your future. In the same way that a football team has a playbook or a theater production has a script, your family mission statement provides direction for you and your family both when you are together and when apart—it becomes a map that provides guidance wherever you go.

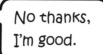

No thanks, I'm good.

As an example, imagine your family mission statement says that drug and alcohol use is unacceptable except where legal and appropriate (i.e. adults having wine with a meal or the use of prescribed medication to treat an illness). In this case, the family mission statement can serve to remind you that you probably don't want to end up at a party where teens are drinking or using other drugs. Certainly we don't expect you to say something as silly as, "No way, dude, my family mission statement forbids the use of drugs and alcohol," but it can serve as a guide that allows you to turn down any offer of alcohol or drugs with a simple, "No thanks, I'm good."

Please don't try to create your mission statement in one burst of effort. We suggest you spend about 10 minutes a week talking with your family over dinner about what everyone thinks should represent your family values. As an alternative, one mom recently shared her family's technique for developing a family values statement, and we loved it so much we want to share it with you.

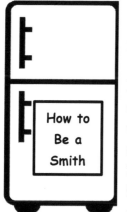

How to Be a Smith

Her idea was to have a huge piece of poster-sized paper taped to the refrigerator door. At the top she put the title, "How to Be a Smith." (Of course, unless your family name is also Smith, you'll want to substitute your name instead.) Everyone in the family was encouraged to write on the paper whatever they thought it meant to be a member of that family. To keep it light and truly focus it on her family, she had written a few funny things on the list to get it started.

For example, since her whole family loves chicken and dumplings, the first entry was, "If you want to be a Smith, you have to love chicken and dumplings." (Once, when Jonathan was presenting our parent meeting with the aid of a translator, we had to stop the meeting because we were laughing so hard when the translator said, in Spanish, "If you want to be a Gonzalez, you have to love menudo.") As the list grew, it came to include much more serious statements about behaviors and beliefs that make a person a Smith, but she never forgot to keep it light from time to time. Here's what a part of our list looks like:

How to Be a Scott:

→ If you want to be a Scott, you have to eat healthy, unprocessed foods most of the time.

→ The Scott family LOVES In-n-Out Hamburgers! (As you can see, there is wiggle room.)

→ To be a Scott, you should be a fan of exercising regularly.

→ The Scott family believes in honesty.

→ If you want to be a Scott, you can't abuse drugs and alcohol.

→ Smoking tobacco is cause for instant dismissal from family membership!

→ The Scott family believes in redemption—you can rejoin the family if you promise to never smoke again!

→ The Scott family LOVES school!

→ To be a Scott, you have to have goals—and a plan to achieve them.

→ Scotts LOVE Disneyland.

Of course, your family mission statement might not look anything like ours, nor should it. Please, though, don't ignore the power of this document. We know—the words "family mission statement" may make your head hurt—but please don't dismiss this just because it sounds hard.

61

Ideas for Your Family Mission Statement:

Find some way to outline and write down your family values.

→ All family members need to be involved in creating this document. If you don't get to help create it, why would you feel bound to follow it?

→ Family values don't change at the front door—they travel with you wherever you go.

2.3 Setting Goals

Everybody wants stuff. Jonathan wants bikes that cost $10,000. Kelly wants to live on the Disney cruise ships. The problem is that just wanting it won't get you any closer to having it.

Wanting things is called dreaming.
Getting things requires something other than dreaming—it's called goal setting.

If you ever want to get to the point where you are able to realize your dreams, you're going to have to learn how to set and achieve goals.

Setting goals is also a critical skill in areas other than simply amassing a big pile of material possessions. In his book *Life Strategies for Teens*, Jay McGraw interviewed hundreds of teens, and one of the most important questions he asked was why each of them had chosen to do or not do drugs. The teenagers who had not done drugs said they didn't because drug use either didn't fit their plans or interfered with important goals they were working toward. The teens who did use drugs said they did so because they were bored and there was no compelling reason not to—in other words, they didn't have any goals.

Goals can open up completely new worlds of achievement and happiness for you, especially if you learn to view them positively and develop the skills necessary to make them work for you. If you want to realize the goals you set, however, you're going to have to follow a few simple guidelines: goals have to be specific, they have to be written down, they have to be measurable, and they have to have a time limit.

They need to be specific. When it comes to making a change, the people who succeed are those who set realistic, specific goals.

"I'm going to recycle all my plastic bottles, soda cans, and magazines" is a much more detailed, achievable goal than "I'm going to do more for the environment." The specific goal will act as a reminder every time you find yourself with an empty bottle or can in your hand, whereas the general goal of helping the environment might not.

<u>They need to be written down.</u> If you don't write them down, goals are painfully easy to forget. If you're trying to cut down on late-night snacking, a big reminder taped to the refrigerator door will work wonders. When that leftover pizza is calling your name, your goal reminder will help silence it.

Remember, though, that when you write a goal down, you should also write why it is important to you, and when you do so, try not to make it about denying yourself something. For Jonathan, it is much more effective to put up a reminder that says, "Do you really want to haul this pizza up that massive hill on your next bike ride?" than it is just to write, "No late night snacks."

They should be measurable. This is very similar to making your goals specific. If you just say, "I want to get good grades," that's a very hard goal to measure. If instead you write, "I want to get at least a 3.8 GPA this semester," you'll automatically be able to tell if you succeeded. It's probably occurred to you that if you are going to be specific about where you want to go (a 3.8 or better GPA), you're going to have to have a plan on how to get there. You don't just get a 3.8 because you're a great person, you get it by averaging all your grades for the semester. If you have good grades in most of your classes but struggle in one specific area, you'll find your biggest potential gains in GPA in that class. If you put together a plan on how you're going to improve in that area (ask your teacher for help, work with a tutor, do extra credit), you have a really good chance of making your goal. If you just keep doing what you've always done and hope for the best, your chances aren't very good.

They should have a time limit. It's obvious why this matters: if you simply write, "I want to get good grades," the question you then have to ask is, "When? Now? In your senior year? When you are in college?" As you can see, the time frame really does make a difference here. When you set a goal, give yourself a time limit within which you should be able to get it done. If you miss your deadline, it's not the end of the world—just establish a new time of completion and do your best to make it happen.

Another way to work with a time limit is to take your desired goal and completion date and then work backward from that point to the present moment. For example, Kelly is an avid participant in the Disneyland 5K, 10K, and half marathon runs. When she signs up for a particular run, she works back from the event date and establishes intermediate performance goals she wants to achieve at specific points. If she follows her plan, she will be totally ready for race day. If the farthest she has walked in the past three months is to the mail box, though, race day is going to be all about suffering.

Put it on your dream board. If the idea of writing everything down freaks you out, there is another way you can put your goals in a concrete form—the dream board. This can be a great tool for younger kids who may not even be able to write yet, but it isn't just for kids—some people, no matter what their age, work better with images than they do with words. The dream board is a vibrant picture collage that represents goals and desires. When our daughter was four, two of her goals were to learn to whistle and learn how to snap her fingers. We did an image search online, found pictures of fingers snapping and lips pursed to whistle, printed them out, and pinned them to the dream board. Within a short time, she had mastered both.

When you achieve your goal, either you can put a date of completion sticker on your board or replace the image with a new one that represents a new goal. Don't throw away the old pictures—stick them in a file. Years later, those old images will bring back powerful memories of what it was like to be you at that

66

age, and they can also serve to remind you how much you have accomplished over the years!

→ Remember that repeating a goal makes it stick.
→ Say your goal aloud each morning to remind yourself of what you want and what you're working for.
→ Every time you remind yourself of your goal, you're training your brain to make it happen.

If you find yourself setting goals so you can please other people, please reconsider. The key to making any change is to find the desire within yourself — you have to do it because you want to, not because a girlfriend, boyfriend, coach, parent, or teacher wants you to. It will be harder to stay on track and energized if you're doing something out of obligation to another person. This isn't selfishness, it's a basic fact about long-term motivation.

If you are new to goal setting, don't get discouraged if you find it difficult at first. It takes time for a change to become an established habit. It will probably take a couple of months before any changes—like getting up half an hour early to exercise—become a routine part of your life. Your brain needs time to get used to this new pattern, but over time it will become so embedded you won't even think about it anymore, you'll just do it. Stick with it—you're on the road to success!

Think About This: Delayed Gratification.

Another positive aspect of goals is that they teach us to delay gratification, a skill that is much more important than it first seems. At the time of this handbook's publication, researchers had recently revisited the subjects of a landmark study on delayed gratification. In the study, the researchers observed the behaviors of children offered a choice: immediately consume a marshmallow, or wait a few minutes and receive a second marshmallow as a reward for waiting.

The children who waited possessed the ability to delay gratification. As the researchers followed the test subjects into their teens, they found that the children who resisted temptation had better self-images, higher levels of self-efficacy, scored higher on their SAT's, and had better relationships with their peers and parents.

The most recent assessment of the test subjects revealed dramatic results. The children who lacked the ability to delay gratification grew up to be adults with the same lack of control, and they also expressed multiple problems associated with impulse control— gambling addiction, drug and alcohol addiction, weight problems, and trouble saving for retirement.

2.4 Treating Consequences Like Goals

When Jonathan and Kelly were young, parents and teachers didn't use the word "consequences." They had other words, like "punishment," "torture," "flogging," and "public humiliation." Today, you have consequences. No matter what word you use, though, what we're talking about is the penalty you have to pay when you mess up.

The funny thing about consequences is they aren't very effective at stopping unwanted behaviors if you don't know what they are until later. Sure, maybe you'll remember that the last time you did this thing—like three months ago—you had to pay a penalty of some sort, but who's to say you'll have to pay that penalty again? Maybe you will, maybe you won't.

There is a way, though, that you can understand ahead of time what the consequences will be for an unwanted behavior: if someone explains them to you beforehand.

Imagine you're thinking about going to a party where some kids in attendance will be drinking. That doesn't mean everyone will be drinking, and it doesn't mean you will necessarily be either—after all, not all kids do drugs (wink, wink—look at the cover if you don't get it).

You really want to go to this party, but you know your parents would have a meltdown if they found out. What will happen if you get caught? Well, unless they've already told you what will happen, you don't know, and that makes you more likely to go to the party. Why?

Because studies have shown that teens are more willing to take a risk if the cost of taking that risk is undefined.

In other words, if you don't know the price of a risk, you are more likely to take it.

This is where the clearly understood consequence comes into play. If, instead, your parents have told you exactly what that decision is going to cost you (and the cost is high), you are less likely to chance it.

So if your parents have taken the time to clearly outline what it is going to cost you if you make a really poor choice, you are less likely to act dumb. **It's simple.**

Or is it? Here's where it gets a little complicated.

If your parents start talking to you about parties and drinking and smoking marijuana, doesn't it sound a little bit like they already think it's going to happen? You might be thinking, "Wait a minute. Why is my dad talking to me about shots of tequila? Is that what he thinks I'm doing? But I'm not doing shots of tequila. Is he saying he thinks I should be? Now I'm all confused!"

70

This is a difficult message
for your parents to get across.

They have to find a way to say:	We hope and expect you will honor our family values by not drinking or using drugs, but we also understand you live in a world where some young people will. If you choose to be one of those people, this is what it will cost you.

Discussing the consequences of use before it happens gives you a chance to change potential behavior in a positive, proactive way. In addition, while it may be hard for your parents to have these kinds of discussions, it helps them as well. Now if you mess up, they will still be disappointed and angry, but they won't have to waste time and energy trying to figure out what to do—they already have a clearly defined course of action.

Here's where it gets really twisted:
Consequences are your friends.

We know that sounds ridiculous, but if you think about it, it's easy to see. Most of the kids we work with are really nice people, and they certainly don't like to disappoint their parents. The problem a lot of them have, though, is they don't know how to get out of a negative situation without looking bad. If, however, you work with your parents to arrange consequences for unwanted behaviors ahead of time, you now have a built-in excuse for getting out of troublesome situations.

One of the hardest things for many of us to do is say no to something other people are doing while still maintaining social status, and it's even harder when everyone is looking at you and the jerk in your group keeps calling you a wimp. If you can look your friends in the eye, though, and say, "Really, I can't—if I get caught, my mom will saw my leg off with a butter knife," you might just be able to dodge this particular challenge. (It also helps if your friends believe your mom would actually follow through on the threat, so tell her to bone up on her acting skills.)

We call the ability to stand up to your friends "being a Neville," after Neville Longbottom from the Harry Potter series. Sure, Hermione slams him with a petrificus totalus spell, but you know what they say: "Petrificus totalus is temporary, but the House Cup is forever." Or something like that.

The major take-away we want you to get here is the idea that the threat of consequences gives you a believable way to deflect the offer of drugs and alcohol. The more tools you have to help you avoid drinking or using drugs, the better off you'll be when socializing with your friends. Consequences can be a great tool, and they can help you be a Neville, too.

One thing you have to realize, though, is that if you're going to develop a list of consequences for certain undesirable behaviors, you will actually have to suffer those consequences if you do, in fact, mess up.

72

Making the punishment fit the crime is one of the hardest things parents and guardians do.

If we overshoot and make the penalty way too strong, we run the risk of inciting a rebellion.

On the other hand, if we make the penalty too soft, we don't extinguish the unwanted behavior, and since we're talking about the use of drugs and alcohol, we definitely want it extinguished.

Think About This: Think Like A Parent
One consequence most kids don't think of until it's too late is how some of their ill-considered actions will affect their parents and families. Breaking the no drugs and alcohol rule is a big deal. It's not like you forgot to take out the trash—you have done something that has the potential to kill you in some cases. Don't just blow that off, by the way. Maybe you don't think of your death as possible or real, but trust us when we tell you your parents do. Unless you can look at it from the perspective of a parent (and you won't be able to until you are one), it's hard to understand why they get so freaked out when it comes to the issue of substance abuse—you could die!

If you get caught, your parents are going to be scared, disappointed, angry, confused, and hurt. By the way, you're not going to be doing all that great, either.

Because all these emotions are going to be running at such a fevered pitch, the potential to overreact is very high. That's why it's such a good idea to determine consequences beforehand. That way, you eliminate (or at least reduce) the chances that someone

73

is going to do or say something hurtful that can't be taken back later.

When you work with your parents to develop consequences that deal with the issue of drugs and alcohol, you should all strive to keep things in perspective. Teen drug and alcohol use is never a small thing, but there will obviously be different levels of transgression. Each subsequent level of rules violation should carry with it a larger penalty.

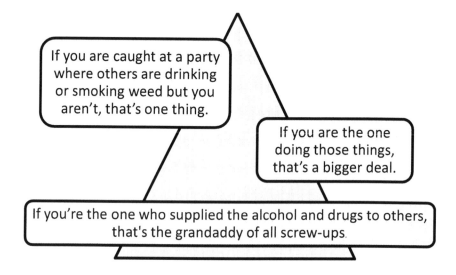

If you are caught at a party where others are drinking or smoking weed but you aren't, that's one thing.

If you are the one doing those things, that's a bigger deal.

If you're the one who supplied the alcohol and drugs to others, that's the grandaddy of all screw-ups.

The question then becomes one of what the consequence should be for each level, and this is where it gets hard.

The main type of consequence we see instituted is for your parents to take something away that you desire or value. You'll eventually get it back after a certain period of time, or you may have to wait until after you display a change in behavior or attitude.

Things they might take away:

→ phones,
→ computers,
→ tablets,
→ video games,
→ musical instruments,
→ favorite clothing items,
→ skateboards,
→ just about anything!

They can also take away something you have been looking forward to:

→ prom,
→ sporting events,
→ vacations,
→ family trips,
→ getting a driver's license,
→ joining a club or team.

 Another area where parents regularly take something away is with your curfew—essentially, they are taking away time. As you can see, the list is extensive.

Unfortunately, taking things away works well for some kids and not at all for others. Many times parents and kids find themselves trapped in an ever-increasing spiral of taking away more and more but realizing fewer and fewer benefits. It's not that taking things away is a bad idea, but it generally doesn't work all by itself.

 Some parents choose to institute consequences by adding responsibility. They may require you to do more around the house, or do volunteer work out in the community.

 In cases where teens are stupid enough to drink and drive—or ride in a car with a drunk driver—some of our parents have had their children attend a Mothers Against Drunk Driving (MADD) victims night, where they hear heartbreaking tales of how drunk drivers shatter the lives of their victims and their victims' families. It is a rare person who emerges from one of these presentations unchanged.

This type of punishment is complicated, since it usually requires that your parents regularly check to see if you are accomplishing your tasks or living up to your community commitments, and in the case of volunteer work, they often are left with the job of schlepping you all over town to get it done. This can get to be more of a punishment for your parents than it is for you, and that's not what this is supposed to be about.

Finally, some parents choose instead to allow for the development of what are called natural consequences. This type of consequence is considered by many to be the best of all the options available, but few parents are willing to go this route because of the harshness and permanence of the costs involved. They are also hard to employ because of the open-ended amount of time it takes for the consequence to show itself.

Natural consequences are direct results brought about by your behavior:
→ If you don't do your homework, you get into trouble at school.
→ If you don't study for a test, you fail the test.
→ If you get arrested, you spend some time in jail.
→ If you use drugs and alcohol, especially when you're young, you run a big risk of assault, injury, dependence, addiction, and death.

When natural consequences are in play, your parents won't spend a lot of time yelling at you about your grades, but neither will they write a check for an expensive college. They won't go all crazy when you get arrested, but they won't bail you out, either. In the end, they will grieve for you when you fall into a pattern of addiction, but they won't lend you money or let you live in their house when your life falls apart as a result. Natural consequences are a beast.

The reason most parents won't let natural consequences run their course is because they understand that you really aren't capable of clearly understanding the long term impact your current bad behaviors can have on your life years later. (Read the section on the teen brain to understand why this is so.) When they save you from experiencing the natural consequences of your behavior, they are literally saving you from yourself.

Unfortunately, when your parents save you from some terrible

fate, they also end up not allowing you to learn the lessons required in order to avoid that same fate the next time.

We hope you are starting to appreciate how complicated consequences are, and what their purpose is. They are not about making you suffer, and they are not about parents gleefully and randomly causing you pain. Consequences serve to warn you about bad behavior and encourage better decisions in the future. If your parents are trying to engage you in a conversation about consequences, try to not roll your eyes and heave huge sighs of exasperation. In fact, if they haven't broached the subject yet, maybe you can be the one to get it started. It might sound like lunacy, but it will actually work out better for you over time if you do.

If you do fall prey to a consequence, don't act like you're the victim—you're not. Part of becoming a mature young adult requires that you be able to own your behaviors. If you are living with a consequence, it is a result of your choices and behaviors, so stand up and own it. They may not admit it, but if you do this, you will impress the heck out of your parents.

All of our conversation about consequences so far has been centered on extinguishing unwanted behaviors and punishing  transgressors, but that is an incomplete picture. What we mean is this: if parents are going to punish bad behavior, they should be just as willing to reward good behavior. One of the basic tenets of motivating people says you get better results by reinforcing desired behaviors than you do punishing undesired ones.

One of Jonathan's old management trainers used to say, "You've got to catch them doing something right!" We think that when your parents catch you doing something right, they should reward you.

Some parents have expressed concern about a system where a child's cooperation is up for sale. That's a valid point, but that's not what we're suggesting. These rewards can take many forms, some material, some more ethereal. Maybe the reward is a statement by your parents of their honest appreciation of your good character, maybe it's the granting of a new right or privilege you've been wanting.

78

This can actually become an excellent way for you to learn how to set goals and achieve them. The reward your parents give you for reaching your goal is just a little motivation to help you get there, and goodness knows we all need a little extra motivation now and then. Just remember that when you set a goal it should be clear, it should be written down, and it should have an end.

We met a mother and daughter team years ago who had this arranged perfectly. The goal was for the daughter to not drink or do drugs, the time frame was six months, and the reward was two tickets to the concert or show of the daughter's choice. Every six months they would sit down and have a short conversation about whether the daughter had achieved her goal. If they agreed she had, she got her reward.

You're probably wondering what would happen if she didn't meet her goal, but they had that covered too. If the daughter failed to meet her goal—if she was caught drinking or using drugs—she would have to go to school for a full year without any makeup. That probably doesn't sound like such a big deal to some of you, but for this girl that would have been the end of her world. That's the thing—goals and rewards have to be personal. If you're going to strive to reach a goal, it has to matter to you or you won't put any effort into it.

What really matters about this story is its outcome: we knew this family for many years, and to the best of our knowledge, the daughter didn't drink or do drugs all the way through college. To us, this represents the perfect illustration of the power of consequences, goals, and rewards. Use them to your advantage; ignore them at your peril.

Lessons Learned: Setting up consequences and rewards can be a win-win situation for you and your family. By setting up consequences for drug and alcohol use in advance, you create a tool that helps you turn down any potential offers of drugs and alcohol. You're protected and your parents are less stressed out, and that's a good deal for everyone.

2.5 To Drug Test Or Not To Drug Test, That Is The Question

 Unless you win the lottery or have a trust fund so big you'll never have to work a day in your life, you're probably going to be drug tested by a potential employer at some point. Actually, you might have to pass a drug test as a qualification for receiving your trust fund, so that just leaves the lottery, and if that's your Plan A, you have a smaller chance of succeeding than you do of getting struck by lightning. Not a good plan.

Like it or not, drug testing is now part of our world. They can test your blood, your urine, and your hair, and the tests are getting more accurate each year. Although the example above referenced employers testing you, it could just as well be a coach, a school board, or a parent asking you to submit to testing as well.

The harsh reality of drug testing is that nobody is going to take you at your word. It doesn't matter what you say—drug testing is all about getting concrete proof that you are innocent or guilty. It is because of that fact that we are not fans of drug testing teens. Since we are such big advocates for relationship building and ongoing communication between parents and their kids, it would be hard for us to recommend something that throws all of that away in one invasive moment of absolute mistrust.

This does not mean that we think that drug testing is useless. Actually, we advocate drug testing in two circumstances:

81

1. The first is quite bleak, and yet it's also pretty rare, so let's just get it out of the way now. If a kid is so out of control, so over the edge that he or she is completely oppositional and defiant and the parents suspect that drugs may be the primary cause of the behavior, then drug testing is completely in order.

When all communication has ceased and trust is completely absent, the parents have to take action. Before they can take any meaningful action, though, they have to know as much as possible  about the situation. Drug testing in this case is the only reliable way they can figure out the depth of the drug issues that are haunting their child's life. It is a desperate situation, and that means it requires desperate measures to deal with it. Drug testing is one of those measures, and in cases like this, we recommend it.

2. The other circumstance where we are comfortable with drug testing is the diametric opposite of the one above. In this case, you and your parents agree that one of the best ways for you to be able to turn down offers of drugs and alcohol is to be able to look your friends in the eye and truthfully say,

I can't you guys— my parents drug test me.

Some people suggest that you don't really even have to be tested, that you can just tell your friends that you are. That's all well and good, but we think the fatal flaw is that you have to lie. We don't think it's healthy to get a job this important done dishonestly. A lot of destruction has had its origin in well-intentioned lies, and we just aren't comfortable recommending that. If you want to use drug testing as a resistance skill, every once in a while, you should be tested.

As an added reinforcement, you can try a technique one of our friends uses. She wants her son's friends to believe him when he says he gets tested, so she purchased the biggest, most outrageous looking drug test kit she could find, and she put it right on the mantle in the middle of their den. When his friends come to visit, they can't help but see it. It's about as subtle as a punch in the face, but it gets the point across beautifully.

As you can see, we are not talking about some random sneak attack. You and your parents are actually on the same team here, so it's not going to be the same as when you are tested like you're a suspect. Let's be very clear, though: this is not your normal day. When you have to hand a little plastic cup of your urine to your mom or dad, it's going to register pretty high on the creepy scale. Either that or you will both be laughing so hard you run the risk of spillage, and that's not good no matter how you spin it!

Ultimately, the goal of drug testing is for you and your parents to do whatever it takes for you to get through your teen years without drinking or using drugs. If drug testing can play a part in getting that job done, we're all for it.

2.6 The Internet

Even with content filters, spam blockers, password protection, and anti-virus programs, the Internet is still the electronic equivalent of the Wild West. Without adult oversight, the Internet can be  dangerous and misleading for you and your friends. While you may be light years ahead of your parents when it comes to technical skills, many of you aren't as worldly as you think you are. We know, pretty insulting, right? Unfortunately, it's alarmingly easy to be misled by slick, professional looking websites that tell you drug and alcohol use is perfectly safe; or by a predator posing as a friendly peer. Of course, you probably think that you'd never be so dumb as to fall for that type of trickery, but remember—every single victim of every single internet scam thought the same thing up until the time they got burned.

Here are a few things to keep in mind when it comes to technology:

→ If you're worried that your parents might look over your shoulder and freak out when they see what it is you are currently viewing, you probably shouldn't be there in the first place. We suggest to parents that internet availability in the home should be communal—there shouldn't be any closed doors between you and your parents when you're online. You probably see this as an invasion of your privacy, but it really is one of the keys to keeping you safe online. This doesn't mean we think adults should be privy to every word you type or say to your friends (necessarily), but they should be able to view your history and not have a seizure. BTW—if your history is always empty, you're guilty of something.

→ You don't need your phone or your iPad while you're sleeping. Really. You don't. We understand that, for many of you, to be without your cell phone feels as if you've lost a limb, but technology that interrupts or delays your sleep is bad for you. Put your chargers somewhere other than your bedroom, and turn off your ringers when you plug your devices in for the night. We tell your parents that nothing good ever happened on a cell phone after 10pm. You know it, and we know it.

→ Take advantage of classes or workshops on internet safety. Anyone with a brain recognizes that an email that starts with the words "Dear Customer" is a ridiculously lame scam, but not all online trickery is this inept. If you feel cocky about your internet skills, you may be setting yourself up for a fall. Avail yourselves of the experts any chance you get.

→ Any time you visit websites that talk about drugs, be very, very careful about believing what they say without question. Unfortunately, this goes for almost all drug websites—both pro and con. Drugs are an issue that polarizes people—they are either rabidly against them or vociferously for them. When reading about drugs online, remember that they are nowhere near as good or safe as the pro-drug websites say they are, nor are they as uniformly and horrifically bad as the anti-drug sites say they are. Websites that tell you there is no consequence if you smoke weed are lying to you. Websites that tell you everyone that smokes weed will end up shooting heroin are lying to you.

85

Here's the thing we want you to keep in mind: there is no safe, healthy, or cost-free use of drugs and alcohol for kids. Period.

→ If you ever read the comments that follow online articles, please remember that the only qualification a person needs to speak there is an internet connection. People who make comments are rarely experts, and statements in the comment section that masquerade as facts are actually just opinions. It's our opinion (but not necessarily a fact) that you will live a full, happy life even if you never read a single comment that follows an article or story online. When it comes to comments, less is usually better.

2.7 Did My Parents Ever Use Drugs?

The number one, by far, hands down, without question, most frequently asked question at our parent presentations has been and will always be,

What should I say if my kids ask me if I ever did drugs?

Most of the questioners fall into one of three groups:

1. The ones who are terrified their kids are going to ask but don't know how to answer.

2. The ones who have already been asked and immediately answered with a big, fat lie.

3. The ones who never used and think they can't answer the question effectively because they feel like total nerds.

 Admittedly, this is a tough question, but the fear it inspires in parents is impressive. Why?

Most of the time, this panic is caused by their concern over what will happen when they answer. If they admit using, will you follow their example? If they deny it, will your trust in them be shattered if you ever find out they lied? Will you dismiss them as irrelevant if they tell you they never did anything?

87

A lot of parents have lost a lot of sleep over this issue, and you may spend more than a little time thinking about it yourself, so let's look at the possible answers parents might give and figure out how to deal with the information they share when they do answer.

The first thing to understand is that even the experts are divided on how to deal with this question. Some say parents should lie about their past use, others advise total honesty, and still others advise avoiding an answer altogether. So, if even the experts disagree over how to answer, how are your parents supposed to get it right? Even more important, though, is how will you benefit the most from whatever information they provide?

We suggest that, no matter what answer they choose, they have to put some thought into it before they respond. Both you and your parents also have to realize that this can't be dealt with once and then put on the shelf—this should be a part of an ongoing substance abuse conversation that continues throughout your relationship.

One very important consideration to keep in mind is the age of the person asking the question. It's hardly ever wise for a parent to discuss his or her drug use with a six-year-old kid. It's not that we're suggesting that parents should just whip out a lie whenever a young child asks an uncomfortable question. Instead, we suggest young children aren't emotionally ready to deal with something as complicated as a parent's past drug use. In this case, we think it would be smart for the parent to simply deflect the question—divert the child's attention elsewhere. In our first book, also titled *Not All Kids Do Drugs*, we suggest that the parent point out the window and excitedly ask, "Is that an eagle!?!" Whatever works, you know?

Another complication parents have to consider (and you have to appreciate) is whether there is a younger sibling present when you drop your bombshell question about their past use. It may be advisable for them to answer the question you have asked, just not at the moment. If you want an honest answer, you're going to have to pay attention to the circumstances within which you ask the question.

You should also understand that if your parents did happen to do drugs at some other point in their lives, they have mixed feelings about appearing hypocritical. The thinking goes like this: they used, but they don't want you to. But if they did it, how can they tell you not to? It just feels wrong. Their confusion, while understandable, is unnecessary.

Here's why:

A hypocrite is a person who says one thing but does another. The reason a parent who used to use drugs can tell his or her child not to without being a hypocrite lies in the fact that the drug use is not occurring any more.

If they used to do something (use drugs) but don't do it anymore, they are not hypocritical when they tell you not to do it. People who learn from experience and share their knowledge are referred to as something entirely different—they are teachers.

Please note, however, that if a parent is currently using drugs while advising a child not to, they are definitively, without doubt a

89

massive hypocrite, and they deserve to be mocked! Not really—no mocking is allowed—but they should be ashamed of their hypocrisy. They should also be aware that their drug use will have a huge influence over whether their child uses. James Baldwin said it best when he said, "Children have never been very good at listening to their elders, but they have never failed to imitate them."

So it's probably best if you just don't ask—what you don't know can't hurt you, right? Nope—wrong. If you're old enough to handle the answer—and if you're reading this book, you probably are—you should ask. You just have to be sure to ask in the right way, you have to help your parents answer effectively, and you have to use the answers as helpful information, not emotional weaponry.

Here's how:
1.   Don't ask until you are ready for the answer.

2.   Don't ask if there are younger siblings in the room; it may not be an appropriate conversation for them.

3.   Assure your parents you are not trying to trap them; you're just trying to understand the challenges and complexities of substance use.

4.   Put your question into context—tell them you are reading a book on the subject, and that the book suggested this might be a helpful conversation.

5.   Give them permission not to answer right away. Let them know you would rather hear the truth, and if that requires some thought on their part, you're comfortable with that.

6. Tell them to share only what they are comfortable sharing. You don't need to know every detail all at once—or ever, for that matter.

7. If they have ever attended one of our parent meetings, they will probably answer by saying, "Yes, I did." They really shouldn't say much more than that at this stage of the conversation, nor should you push them to get into all the juicy details. If your response to their affirmative answer is to freak out, stop here and try again in a few years (when you've grown up a little). Pointing fingers and tearfully accusing your parents of being drug addicts is not going to be helpful.

8. Let them explain how this ended up happening. It may be hard to believe, but your parents were young once, and they were probably as confused by their worlds as you are by yours. Realize that drug education is a relatively new subject in schools—your parents may have not had any education at all except what they heard from other kids, and listening to what other kids said about drugs back then was worse than no education—it was rumor and bad information masquerading as fact. Also, keep in mind that many of today's illegal drugs were legal just a few decades ago—and not like marijuana is legal in a few states right now (for people 21 and older), but just plain legal for anyone, no matter what their age. Remember, too, that drugs are purer and more powerful today. Of course, that doesn't make their use right, but it does make your possible use more dangerous.

9. Finally, let them tell you why they stopped. Maybe they just got bored, or maybe the promises drugs offered ended up being empty. As weird as it sounds, you may be the reason your parents stopped using drugs. You see, it's hard being a good parent, but it's almost impossible to be a good parent while high. We love the sound of the reason some parents give their children for stopping drug use: "I stopped because I had you, and I only wanted to give you my best." Many times, it's true, and if it is, it's a really powerful thing for your parents to be able to tell you.

As we said earlier, it is totally unfair to use this information as a weapon against your parents. They are struggling to be honest with you, and in the future, they may not be so willing if you take their honesty and throw it back in their faces. Open communication with your parents as you progress through high school is critical, but you have to act like a human being if you want it to happen.

In some cases, your parent will answer your "Did you use?" question by saying, "No, I never did."

Please appreciate that many times parents who never used actually think that fact disqualifies them from being able to help you resist drug use. Many parents who didn't use in high school still remember that their non-use often felt unpopular and uncool.

After two decades of being drug educators, we can tell you that this phenomenon is something we are just sick to death of. Non-users are not losers—that's a lie people who drink and do drugs repeat over and over again so they can feel good about the mistakes they are making.

The fact that so many nice, smart, interesting young people fall prey to it really bothers us. People who choose to not use drugs shouldn't feel bad about that decision—that ship needs to be sunk.

Help your parent to realize this truth. If they say they never used, please tell them, "Cool. Maybe you could help me do that, too." It may take a few minutes for the look of shock to subside, but when it does, they may have some valuable lessons to share with you. Let your parents know that geek is the new hip—they have finally arrived!

One last point: If, in your discussions, your parents tell you the reason they never used was a result of addiction or alcoholism on the part of a parent or close relative, make sure you understand that this will directly affect you. If this is the case, please refer to section 1.6, where we discuss the potential for family addiction or alcoholism to be inherited. If you have this risk factor, you need to know the great power it has over your future if you choose to drink or do drugs, especially if you do so when you are young.

Part 3
Life Is A Series Of Conversations

3.1 What Is Positive Proactive Language?

Some kids abuse drugs and alcohol. The first question everyone seems to ask is, "Why?" Our answer to this is also one of our core philosophies:

Drugs aren't the problem, they are a symptom of another problem that isn't being dealt with in a better way.

It is our opinion that a lot of drug and alcohol abuse is the result of people never being taught how to deal with a handful of common problems.

One of these basic problems happens when negative language dooms us to failure by polluting our attitudes with an "I can't" outlook. The solution? Learn how to communicate with what is called "positive proactive language." We know, for some of you, the name is almost a deal breaker—it just has that deep taste of self-help mumbo jumbo, and that makes it a perfect lesson in understanding how you can use it in your life if you're just willing to buy in.

Kelly loves terms like positive proactive language. She is so terminally upbeat, so…..positive, she can't wait to hear about the wonderful promise that phrases like this hold. When Jonathan was younger, these words would have put him instantly on guard. Phrases like positive proactive language made him want to gouge his eyes out, set himself on fire, and throw himself off a cliff in a moment of Anthony Bourdain-esque panic. Which of the two of us do you think ended up as the drug addict and alcoholic? Correct.

Because Jonathan spent so much of his life seeing the bad in things, he also spent a good portion of that life reacting poorly to situations that he unfailingly read as negative—despite the fact that they usually were not. There is nothing inherently wrong with the three words "positive proactive language." The fault lay in how Jonathan reacted to them. All that negativity, all that playing the victim are what made drug and alcohol use that much easier for him. When you always see the bad, you frequently end up having to reach for quick fixes in order to feel good.

Since Kelly already sees the good, she doesn't have to use artificial means to feel good, and that is the secret power of positive proactive language. When you change **"can't"** language into **"can"** language, you can turn a situation that seems negative into a positive. You can establish control over how you see situations, and this sense of self-direction can benefit you when dealing with offers of drugs and alcohol at parties. By the way, you can do this. If Kelly can teach Jonathan how to stop seeing the bad in everything, you can learn how to do it too.

First you have to decide if you need to change.

Try this short test to see what kind of language you use in your daily life. It will quickly become apparent to you if you regularly employ positive proactive language.

Pick the one phrase from each pair that most closely mirrors what you might say:

→ "I can do this," or, "I'm not sure I can do this."
→ "I can do a cartwheel, if I just practice enough," or, "I tried it once, and I fell. I can't do cartwheels."
→ "I can make this work," or, "I don't think this will work."
→ "Let's look at all the options," (Kelly's favorite phrase) or, "I have to do it this way. This is the way I've always done it."
→ "I can add and subtract, but I'll need help if I want to get better at multiplication and long division," or, "I'm just not good at math."
→ "If we work hard, prioritize, plan, and save, we can go on the vacation we want," or, "We could never afford a cruise like that."
→ "Smoking is an addiction, and it will be hard to stop at first, but other people have done it, so I can do it too!" or, "I always fail when I try to quit. I must have an addictive personality."

If you predominantly chose the first option, you are a **positive, proactive person**. You have confidence that things will work out if you work at them (you are positive), and you take action in anticipation of future problems or needs that may crop up (you are proactive).

If you found yourself identifying more often with the second phrase, you are **negative and reactive**. Not only do you have very little hope anything is possible (you are negative), but you are always the victim of circumstances you see as being beyond your control (you are reactive).

Reactive language is much more than just saying, "I can't," in any given situation. It is the strong internal sense that you are powerless over that situation and nothing you do will change the outcome. It is not only the language of victimization and persecution, but also the language of absolutes, like "you always" and "you never" statements.

If you are a reactive thinker, you'll often sound like this:

→ "Why don't you ever listen?"
→ "You always… (Fill in the blank.)"
→ "There's nothing I can do about it. That's just the way I am."
→ "I'd like to, but I just don't have the time."
→ "That's just the way boys/girls are."
→ "Why do you always blame me?"
→ "Why do you always make such a mess?"
→ "All kids are going to drink alcohol sooner or later."

97

Reactive people have a feeling of being out of control, and reactive language creates an atmosphere of powerlessness, failure, and blame. It doesn't take a lot of imagination to see how the frustration and stress caused by constant negativity and reactive thinking could lead to alcohol and drug use in an effort to stop feeling so awful all the time. It doesn't have to be that way.

When you learn to view situations as changeable and controllable, rather than as destiny, you will come to see that there are always multiple options when dealing with any given situation, and this will give you the confidence to be in charge of your direction and development.

Lessons Learned: Positive Proactive Language

→ Positive proactive language makes for healthy communication and encourages responsibility.
→ You may have been deeply conditioned to be reactive, but you can change with awareness and effort.
→ Perspective is everything. The same situation is either controllable or controlling—it's all in how you see it.
→ Find another way to say it, and you can create a new way to do it!
→ Proactive people are ready for the curve balls that life throws them, in that they are flexible and open to new ways of getting the job done.

3.2 Listening—An Art And A Skill

Lately, it seems like many people are under the impression that communication consists of them talking. We know you're waiting for more, but that's all there is. Tune in to any cable news program and watch how the political talking heads interact with each other—neither party puts much stock in listening to what their opponent is saying. Instead, they spend the majority of the time rudely talking over each other. The default position seems to be the loudest voice wins, and the act of listening is a sign of weakness. That may represent something, but it certainly isn't communication.

The old saying, "You have two ears and one mouth—use them proportionally," is kind of silly (yes, you have two ears, but they are linked to only one brain), but it does suggest a healthy model for good communication. If we listen well, the act of communicating is much more completely realized, for communication is a two-way street made up of both speaking and listening.

How does this have anything to do with drugs and alcohol?
Well, if you buy into the idea that strong relationships with family, friends, teammates, coaches, and teachers lessen the chance that young people will use, it becomes instantly apparent that communication plays a big part in forming those bonds. Since we've already agreed that listening is at least half of communication, it's easy to see that listening plays an important role in drug and alcohol resistance skills.

Think about how you listen to people. Do you value what they are saying, or are you much more concerned with what you are going to say when they finish whatever it is that they are droning on about?

When you listen:

→ Are you busy thinking of what you're going to say next while ignoring what is currently being said?

→ Do you find yourself nodding you head in agreement when you actually couldn't say what the person speaking is talking about if your life depended on it?

→ Do you find yourself spacing out—actually coming out of a fog to the realization you have no idea how long it's been since you've heard a word the speaker said?

→ Do you find yourself finishing other people's sentences for them, since you already know what they are going to say?

→ Are you engaged in a secondary activity, like flipping from screen to screen on your phone or checking the ESPN crawl on the television across the room?

→ Are you letting past experiences with the speaker prejudice what you're hearing and interpreting?

If you see yourself in any of the above examples, you need some remedial listening therapy. Maybe you've forgotten how, or maybe you were never taught how, but you are a terrible listener! Despair not, however. Listening, like any other skill, is one you have the ability to learn. Once you determine that you need some help to become a good listener, all you need are a few suggestions, the willingness to change, and practice, practice, practice (you might even get to Carnegie Hall).

A few listening tips:

→ When listening, just listen. After the speaker is done, take a moment to reflect on what was said, and then formulate your response based upon the entirety of what was said, not just the first few words or sentences.

→ If you need to, jot down a key word or two during long statements so you don't have to devote a part of your awareness to holding an important point in your head the whole time.

→ Repeat back what it is you think was said. If you missed the point, have the speaker restate his or her thoughts in another way so you might better understand.

→ Try to remember that if someone has chosen to speak to you, what he or she is speaking about is probably important to him or her. Show that they are important to you by listening.

Lessons Learned: Listening

Everyone wants to be heard. By listening to your parents, friends and family, you send the message that you care what is going on in their lives. If you want truly to communicate with someone, you have to hear what he or she is saying. Remember, your goal is to communicate effectively with all the people in your life. The strong bonds forged in communicative relationships make you better able to resist the temptations of drugs and alcohol.

3.3 Self-Talk

If you ever get the chance to spend any time around a 3 to 5-year-old kid, you'll notice that they often talk to themselves out loud. When they do, you probably don't immediately leap to the conclusion, "This kid is nuts!"

On the other hand, if you were walking down the street and you came upon an adult who was doing the same thing, you'd steer clear of them, since they obviously suffer from some sort of mental illness.

There really isn't much difference between what we see as a "normal" kid and a "disturbed" adult—everybody talks to himself or herself. The only real difference is that by the time we leave early childhood, most of us have learned not to do it aloud. From about the age of six, people still talk to themselves all the time, they just do it in what is called self-talk, inner speech, or the internal monologue.

Why should you even care? First, you have to realize that this internal monologue is going on almost all the time. Depending on what tone it takes, though, it can make you feel either fantastically good or disastrously awful. When something that powerful is going on in your mind almost all the time, it kind of matters that you be aware of it and make changes to it when necessary.

If your inner voice is constantly telling you your body is unattractive, your self-image and self-esteem are taking a constant beating. If allowed to continue, this insulting inner monologue can go so far as to inspire eating disorders and pathological body dissatisfaction. It requires a conscious choice to fight these self-defeating messages, but until we actually identify the destructive message and take conscious action to change it, we will continue to be victimized by it.

Author Chick Moorman wrote about "I am's" as an important tool for building self-esteem as kids grow up. He refers to "I am's" as core beliefs children express about themselves.

When they make statements such as we see above, people establish and build positive self-regard. On the other hand, "I am fat" and, "I am ugly" can only hurt anyone who speaks them internally (or externally, for that matter). As you can see, the way we refer to ourselves is extremely important in determining how we see ourselves: **positively or negatively.**

Notice also that this inner speech is a powerful tool you can use to resist your brain when it comes up with a really bad idea. You are probably already aware that not every idea that pops into your head is a great one. Some of what our minds suggest we do is

103

downright self-destructive. If you don't realize that you have the power to resist these urges, you will fall prey to them constantly.

As an example, consider when your brain suggests you get something to eat. It's when you try to decide what you're going to eat that the inner monologue kicks in. Foods like pizza, potato chips and ice cream often get top billing on our brains' menu suggestions, yet if we succumbed to them every time they occurred almost every one of us would have Type 2 diabetes end up in early graves.

The brain's ability to talk to itself allows us to resist unhealthy urges, but it doesn't have any power until we give it voice (well, until we give it inner voice). You won't be able to resist any urge until you realize that other options exist, and you won't choose the healthy option unless health matters to you. All of this gets decided via the use of inner speech.

What you have to realize is that this same battle occurs whenever your brain suggests you drink or do drugs. The major reason people use or abuse substances is because they have the ability to change how we feel, and they do it quickly and powerfully. If you feel physical or emotional pain, drugs appear to offer an easy solution—take them, and the negative feelings go away.

The positive inner voice, if a person allows it to speak, will argue that while drugs may work sometimes, even when they do, it is at great cost. It points out that the consequences of drinking or doing drugs can include auto accidents, arrests, parental disapproval, heartbreak, hangovers, overdoses, embarrassment, violence, addiction, and injury.

The inner voice also has the power to suggest alternative ways to change the way you feel. Many people have negative feelings, and some feel the urge to deal with them quickly and easily, but they counter that urge by telling themselves that running, biking, surfing, meditating, or just talking to a friend will have the same result without all the high costs.

The inner voice's ability to suggest alternatives to urges makes it a powerful tool when it comes to resisting the temptations of drugs and alcohol.

Finally, the inner monologue is where we do almost all of the work associated with decisions about right and wrong. If the opportunity arises for you to steal money or valuables from an unsuspecting friend, you would probably resist that urge because you know deep down that it is just wrong.

If instead you found a large amount of cash on the sidewalk, you might have a harder time resisting the urge to keep it. At that point, your inner voice would help you decide, and it would be your sense of what's right and what's wrong that guided the conversation.

You might think:

Hey, if this person is that careless, they deserve to lose it. Maybe it will teach them to be more careful next time.

OR: I wonder if this money means the difference of life or death for the person who lost it. What if it was for medicine for a sick child? They may have reported the loss to the police— that way, I could give it back to them. How would I feel if I lost this much cash?

It would seem that the inner monologue has another name we haven't mentioned yet: **your conscience**. Often, when we don't listen to our conscience, we end up feeling bad, and then the next battle we may have to fight is the urge to fix our feelings with drugs and alcohol.

The big point we want you to understand is this:

Your actions and feelings follow the tone and quality of your inner speech, and the messages your inner speech sends you can be changed through conscious choice.

If you don't like how you feel, change the way you talk to yourself. If you make the choice to be aware of how you talk to yourself, you gain the power to change that talk if it needs changing. When you do that, you become the master of your world. Who doesn't want that? Start listening to yourself in your head. If you wouldn't let someone else talk to you in a certain way, why would you ever choose to do it to yourself?

 **Lessons learned**: We all talk to ourselves. When we reduce negative self-talk and replace it with positive, we reduce stress and improve self-image and self-esteem. Low stress people with high levels of self-regard are much less likely to drink or do drugs.

106

3.4 Laughter

One of the greatest attributes humans possess is the ability to laugh. To hear a person let loose a wild, unrestrained peal of laughter is a gift of unimaginable value. The old quote about laughter being the best medicine has been shown to be accurate, at least to the extent that it is good for your health.

What each person finds funny, though, is different, so we can't really tell you where to find humor. Jonathan is a fanatical stand-up comedy fan. Kelly has a fantastic eye for humor in the theater. Our 11-year-old daughter is currently at the stage where she experiences great joy in finding and creating puns. Some of you may relish the comedy found in graphic novels, others may spend time viewing the incredible amount of material on YouTube and other online video formats. Whatever form it takes, appreciate the fact that there are almost limitless sources of humor available to you. We encourage you to seek them out and take advantage of the therapeutic value of a good laugh.

A quick word of caution, though—while we don't want to get all preachy on you, we'd like to suggest that humor found at the expense of others is a tricky game to play. Certainly human misfortune is a ripe source of comedy, but if you can only laugh when others are hurting, it could end up being a pretty toxic source of comic relief. It's just something to keep in mind.

People who laugh a lot are healthier, have less stress, and worry less than those who don't. Knowing how to laugh is not just about having a good sense of humor, though. Kids of all ages should also learn how to laugh at themselves. None of us is going to get through this world without doing some incredibly silly and embarrassing things, so if you can laugh at the situation—laugh at your essential humanity—you will be able to forgive yourself the *faux pas* while also getting a good chuckle at the same time. People who can laugh at themselves can move on after they make mistakes, and they have lower levels of stress than the people who suffer the agony of replaying embarrassments repeatedly in their minds.

I can't believe I just said that!

Lessons Learned: Laughter

This is the most enjoyable thing you will do in this whole book—lighten up, and get a good chuckle at the hilarity of being human. Life is just too hard not to.

Part 4
Inside Your Brain

4.1 Why Are Brains So Difficult?

Just about everybody agrees that the human brain is wondrous and amazing, and yet here is the essential irony of the brain: it stores everything we know, and yet most people know almost nothing about it! It is the most phenomenal and miraculous bit of tissue in the universe, but almost everyone is bored to tears by information concerning it.

Here's the conclusion we've come to: we can write all day about dendrites and neurons and brain development and neurotransmitters, and guess what—you're not going to read it. It isn't that it's not important—you just don't have the time, and a lot of you just don't find it interesting.

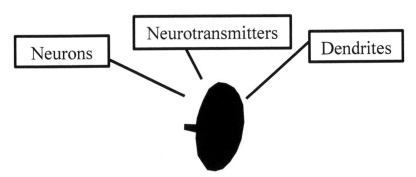

So, **what we're not going to do** is waste all of our time.

What we are going to do is tell you what we think is of the utmost importance:

→ Your brain is currently going through its final developmental stage.

→ The opportunity to learn the skills associated with the PFC (Prefrontal Cortex) is limited—it will be less possible over time to learn the lessons of youth.

→ Your brain is at a point where it overvalues reward and undervalues risk.

→ Drugs and alcohol can devastate you at this vulnerable time.

Please take the time to do this minimal exploration of the most amazing biological entity known to us—our brains.

Authors' note: If you do happen to be one of the few who find information about the brain as fascinating as we do, get in touch with us at our website (the address is on the back cover) and we'll send you the entire brain section we developed for our book *Where's The Party?* There is no charge for this information. If you want it, we want you to have it. You just have to ask.

Your brain is currently going through its final developmental stage.

Ok, first things first. Your brain has been on a developmental building boom since before you were born. Certainly, it has been more active at some points than at others, but the development has been ongoing for more than a decade, and you still have another decade to go before you are done.

The area you are currently developing most aggressively is called the Prefrontal Cortex, or PFC. When it finally reaches full function, it conducts the business of inhibition, impulse control, planning, and problem solving. It is also responsible for decision-making, risk measurement, stress regulation, working memory, and the ability to read emotions, especially the emotions observed in facial expressions.

The PFC links cause and effect—it is the part of the brain that, if it is working as it should, screams "STOP!" when you are about to do something fabulously stupid. Because this area is so closely associated with impulse control, a lack of development here means you have a serious inability to control urges, resist temptation, and manage risk.

Famous PFC saying #1:

"STOP! That's the worst idea you've ever had!!"

Obviously, a brain that lacks the full ability to do all of these important jobs is a brain that can get you into a load of trouble before you even realize a threat exists. This does not in any way indicate that you are stupid or incapable of amazing feats—it just means you have trouble managing impulses and predicting how your current actions will affect you in the future. You should note that your PFC function is diminished even more when you are in the presence of your friends.

111

The opportunity to learn the skills associated with the PFC is limited.

The old saying that "practice makes perfect" has been replaced with a new one: "practice make permanent." Your brain is currently at a stage where it will be directly and permanently changed by what environments you expose it to.

You do not have limitless time to learn how to be an adult. If you practice decision-making and impulse control now, you will be better at those things when you are an adult than you will be if you spend all day getting high and playing video games.

At a certain point, typically as you enter your twenties, your brain will start to become less open to wiring new skills. You will start to lose a good bit of your potential to form new connections in your PFC. If you haven't done the work of growing up by then, you may never fully realize your potential.

Your brain is at a point where it overvalues reward and undervalues risk.

It's amazing how perfectly suited teenage brains are for the work that is laid before them. Think about the biological and social mandates you will face in the coming decade:

Leave home.
Find a mate.
Find food.
Find shelter.
Protect what is yours.

All of these require you to take risks, explore new worlds, and develop new relationships. If you are to succeed, you have to head out into the world, seek new experiences, and above all, take risks. It would seem, then, that risk taking is a behavior that must be richly rewarded, since it is a survival skill. Risk taking is seen by the brain, on some levels, as highly desirable.

This is why teenagers get pleasure when they experience new situations, meet new people (especially ones that are sexually attractive!), and take risks. It is an absolute fact that teens  experience pleasurable changes in brain chemistry when they are in novel situations. It is for this reason that parties are so attractive to you: they offer all of these elements in one neat package.

Unfortunately, there are many land mines waiting for an eager teenager seeking sensation in today's world. Since novel situations result in pleasure, that means you are usually going to see any new situation as attractive; and you will often seek new experiences solely because they are new. Since you aren't very good at predicting what consequences might result from your actions (it's that underdeveloped PFC, remember), new situations can deteriorate rapidly. Instead of taking a moment to figure out if a new behavior will result in a good outcome or a poor one, you will often jump feet first and wait until later to assess the quality of the results.

Drugs and alcohol can devastate you at this vulnerable time.

One of the unfortunate aspects of teen parties we discuss numerous times in this book is that they frequently feature the use of drugs and alcohol.

When teens use drugs and alcohol, they can fall prey to the effects those drugs have on brain function. A teen under the influence of alcohol is less inhibited, less fearful, less reasonable, less committed to his or her normal moral code, has poorer judgment, and can sometimes experience spikes in aggression. In other words, a teen who normally would be very unlikely to take untoward risks can almost instantly become a high-level risk taker just because of the presence of alcohol in the body.

The other problem we have to come to terms with is exactly what developmental message is delivered to a teen brain when a child regularly infuses it with alcohol. A brain that is exposed to alcohol in this manner will quickly start to adapt to the presence of that alcohol—it has to develop in such a way as to incorporate the presence of alcohol into its operating system.

Unfortunately, these changes may make the brain think it cannot operate without alcohol in the future.

 Teens who drink alcohol regularly have a much higher risk of alcoholism in adulthood, and other drugs show similar patterns of a heightened risk of addiction following teen use. Alcohol use by teens has a more pronounced negative effect on memory and learning than a similar dose would in an adult. These memory deficits directly affect academic performance, and they may last for a lifetime.

Teen drinking results in a diminishment in hippocampal size in teens. Evidence exists that after heavy alcohol use—such as what teens experience during spring break style binges—the cells in the hippocampus die off at an astronomical rate when the flow of alcohol ceases, and these damaging effects may never repair themselves.

Adolescents do not get sleepy when they drink, nor do the slur their words or experience the coordination deficits as early as adults do when they drink. Because of this, teen drinkers frequently underestimate how drunk they are and continue to drink well past the point where they do damage to their brains. They are also more likely to attempt things they now have no ability to do safely, like drive a car or make decisions about sexual activity.

Teen brains experience damage from alcohol use in doses that would not harm an adult brain. Remember, teen brains are deep in the process of developing, and because of this, they are extremely sensitive to damage caused by drug and alcohol use during this time.

As bad as alcohol is for teen brains, other drugs do them no favors either. Smokers who start in their teens become much more deeply addicted to tobacco than smokers who start as adults. Unfortunately, almost all smokers start when they are teens.

Nicotine is one of the only drugs that can cause the brain to create more receptor sites for it to occupy, and this effect is more evident in teens. With each new receptor site created, craving for nicotine goes up and the addiction becomes more powerful. Teens who smoke run a serious risk of addiction and all the disastrous health consequences associated with tobacco use, but because their brains are so ill equipped to understand the price of this decision, they end up starting smoking anyway.

One last thing to think about when you are contemplating the effects of drugs on your developing brain—smoking marijuana is not harmless to the teen brain. With each passing day, new studies are being published that show the far-reaching effects smoking weed has on developing teen brains.

While it is true that marijuana is currently legal in two states and will probably be legal in a few more after the 2014 election cycle,  teens cannot use the drug legally or safely. Because of the legalization process, marijuana is being studied more often and more completely than it has in decades, and the news for teens is not good.

Not only does marijuana appear to have profound effects on your ability to learn, remember, and develop adult social skills, it also has been implicated in addiction and neurocognitive damage. As more research in funded in the coming years, the news will only get worse when it comes to teen use and the effects it has on their brains. Please don't fall prey to the temptation to give weed a pass simply because a few states have voted to legalize it. In this case, legal does not mean safe.

As you can see, our new understanding of the teen brain increasingly indicates that it is no longer possible to use the words "teen use" and "safe use" in the same sentence. Since teenagers' brains are at a point where they are easily susceptible to damage, we now understand that teen drug and alcohol use is a direct threat to young people's physical health and mental well-being.

The importance of this cannot be overstated. The world is not kind to people who miss developmental opportunities. Both teens and young adults (and their parents) need to understand that they are laying down the foundation that will make them the adults they will become—they are building the house they will live in for the rest of their lives.

Lessons Learned: The brain is so complex that it actually intimidates us. It's like some sort of sick joke—the thing that makes us so amazing is the very thing that also gives us an inferiority complex!

117

Think About This: The Miracle That Is The Brain

The human body starts out as just two cells, but at birth the brain will be made up of about 75-100 billion cells. Each of those 100 billion cells connect to other cells that surround them or work in concert with them—some estimates put the average number of connection points per brain cell at about 10,000, which means there are about one quadrillion points of contact between the cells in just one human brain.

The brain is a massive consumer of energy. Weighing in at just three pounds, the average brain comprises only 2.5-3% of the body's weight, and yet it consumes around 20% of the body's energy reserves. The brain's demand for oxygen is also quite dramatic. We can last weeks without food; days without water; but only about four minutes need to pass before a lack of oxygen causes brain damage or death. This becomes more important when we discuss how drugs and alcohol can depress respiration and realize the deadly consequences of vomiting while unconscious due to the effects of drugs or alcohol.

4.2 Peer Pressure: The World's Most Misunderstood Term

Peer Pressure Rule Number One: If you want to be accepted by a group, you will always be required to act or think in ways that that the group deems appropriate. Don't misunderstand—you will not be handed an instruction sheet outlining the required behaviors and beliefs. In fact, the members of the group may not even be able to vocalize what it is you are supposed to do—they just know it when they see it. In addition, just to make it more confusing, group acceptance is often less about what you are supposed to do and more about what you are not supposed to do.

Here's what we mean: Go to any political gathering, support the opposing party's agenda, and see how much acceptance that generates. Join the football team, and then burst into tears every time you get hit. Audition for a play, and then break character every time you're onstage. There are many different ways to be politically active, there are a number of methods to deal with pain on an athletic field, and there are dozens of variations on how to deliver a line in a play—all these things are allowed, and the group will still accept you. Do a couple of specific things, though, and you will be rejected.

Add to this the fact that peer pressure is not a single issue—it can exist within an almost limitless number of contexts: drugs and alcohol, sex, academics, cheating, race, athletics, fashion, music, cars, hairstyles, honesty, religion, politics, family issues, employment, materialism, and so on. All of us feel the pressure to fit in, and this pressure comes at us from a thousand different directions.

119

 One thing we want to dispense with immediately is the version of peer pressure parents frequently ask about. It usually starts when they say, "What about the kids at school who are trying to make my son/daughter drink and do drugs?" Let's be clear—one challenge you are not going to have to spend a lot of time dealing with in middle and high school is dodging the free weed guy. It is highly unusual to see or hear about one teen trying to force another to drink alcohol or smoke marijuana. Peer pressure is usually more subtle than that.

It is much more likely to happen like this: You enter a party, and you almost immediately notice that many people are drinking and a number of them are getting high. While you may not necessarily be aware of it, your brain is automatically reminding you of certain rules, and in this case, the most important rule is that the best way to join any group is to do whatever it is that group is currently doing.

Your brain will be very powerfully suggesting that you do what the group is doing, and that's a big problem. Notice that nobody has insisted that you drink, and nobody is forcing you to smoke weed, but if you are going to remain at this party for long, you're much more likely to join in than you would be if you didn't enter. (For more on this, see section 5.3 on how to assess a party.)

This is the big challenge of peer pressure—when the behaviors required for entry clash with your sense of right and wrong. You are going to have to decide if you want to mortgage your personal beliefs in order to gain entry into a group. This is hard, and it's not something a lot of young people have had much practice doing. Remember, the group is not insisting you do anything—

this battle is happening exclusively in your head. Peer pressure, then, almost always comes from within.

Here's how it's usually going to play out: You enter an environment, survey the landscape, choose the group you want to be a part of, and then imagine which behaviors would most quickly allow you entry into that group.

It's important to note that peer pressure is not just about drug and alcohol use at parties. The required behaviors are going to vary widely from group to group and setting to setting.

Think about it. Maybe you know of one group at your school that greets its members in a loud, boisterous, over-the-top way anytime a member arrives. Hugs and kisses all around is normal behavior. Now think about a different group, in which the accepted greeting for newly arriving members is a quick glance, maybe an imperceptible nod of the head, and single word acknowledgement like, "Dude." Now take one member from each group and put them into the other group. How long do you think it will be before the greeting behaviors of the swapped members come under fire? About two seconds.

Here's what we want you to remember about peer pressure—it is subtle, it is constant, it usually comes from within, it is overwhelmingly powerful, and it is present in almost every social situation. Peer pressure is rarely one kid trying to force another to do something. Instead, it is the pressure to conform when in the presence of your peers.

The most important thing to remember about peer pressure, though, is that it is not necessarily bad for you. Whether it has a positive or negative influence on you is almost entirely dependent upon where you choose to spend your time and which group's favor you want to win. In other words, what type of peer pressure you are going to experience is in your hands—you just might not have realized it yet.

Peer Pressure Works Both Ways – Positive Peer Pressure

One of the greatest features of our jobs as drug educators is that our travels expose us to some of the best academic students in the country. The schools we work with offer stellar faculties, fabulous campuses, outstanding technical resources and are blessed with the freedom to admit students who have shown a past ability and continued desire to succeed academically.

Because of this, the academic climate at these schools is almost exclusively one of success; and this is not just the expectation of the faculties and the parents, it is also that of the students.

This leads to a lot of peer pressure to succeed academically, and we are not referring to the high stress, gut-wrenching fear of failure some people suffer under the weight of such expectations. These are students with established records of accomplishment and success, and most of them thrive in this climate. If circumstances arise where a student struggles academically, resources are available to put that student back on a path to success.

For the student who goes a different way, though, the outcome will be decidedly different. Any student who decides academic achievement no longer matters will almost immediately feel stress, because this failure to adhere to the norms of academic success observed by his or her peers will quickly push him or her to the fringes. This falling out with the student's peers may be the force that motivates him or her to get back into the academic mainstream—it may be what rescues them from failure.

The same is true for any group of young people who offer a positive influence to other kids. Our daughter is utterly in love  with theater—the music, the stories, the costumes, the backstage crafts, the actors— you name it. If it has anything to do with theater, she thinks it is magical. Our experience over the past few years has been that the kids she meets when she is involved with putting on a play are generally kind, talented, hardworking and above all, positively influential peers.

Almost every one of them does well in school, and the parents of most of these kids are committed to the idea that if their children want to continue to have the freedom to participate in the productions they must maintain their grades in school and stay out of trouble the rest of the time. In our opinion, that is a decidedly outstanding peer group.

The other great thing about theater is that in order to get up on a stage and deliver lines effectively, actors have to take risks; they have to put themselves out there in a vulnerable, emotional, thrilling way. For most of the kids we've talked to, it's a rush for them to do so; and it's our opinion that if a boy or a girl can get a

123

dopamine and adrenaline surge from being on stage, they're less likely to feel the need to get it by abusing drugs and alcohol.

Peers can have positive effects on each other in less direct ways as well. One of the most powerful protective factors you can have in a difficult social situation is the presence of at least one other like-minded friend. This friend does not have to speak out; in fact, he or she does not have to speak at all. Simply by knowing the other supportive friend is in the room, you can draw strength from his or her presence. Really, this is nothing more than the magic of knowing you are not alone.

 Other examples of positive peer pressure abound, and many of them revolve around sports. While professional and college sports are riddled with stories of drug and alcohol use, and while the athletes who play these sports sometimes seem to suffer a complete lack of maturity and life skills, there are numerous other stories about how athletes use their sport as a way to stay sober, motivated, in school, goal-oriented, and team-centered.

One last story on the many different ways peer pressure exerts its power: For most of her young life, our daughter was too afraid to go on Splash Mountain at Disneyland. That all changed when a friend of hers said, "Come on. I'll go with you. I love this ride!" While both our efforts to get her to go on the ride had failed, her friend's suggestion that they go was much more powerful. Why is it so different?

First, our daughter knows she doesn't have to go on a silly amusement park ride in order for us to love her. She knows there is not one chance in a million we would reject her—ever—no matter what the issue. There is no such guarantee on the part of her friend, however. Of course, it's silly to say that one kid would reject another over a ride, but it's also silly to imagine that our daughter didn't want to win the favor of her friend—she wanted to behave in a way that allowed her to join the group (in this case, a group of one, but that matters not).

In the end, she got on the ride, and she loved it. Her friend never once tried to force her to go—as we said, peer pressure is much more subtle than that—but it was the friend's presence and our daughter's desire to join her that made it happen.

Any attempt to define peer pressure as either good or bad is overly simplistic—it is both. If peers are present, though, peer pressure is present as well.

Some Final Thoughts On Peer Pressure
As you can see, peer pressure can work both ways, negatively and positively. It is usually the pressure you feel to conform when you are with your peers. When you have to violate your personal beliefs in order to conform, the choice becomes much more difficult and stressful. If you don't value yourself and your beliefs more than you value the acceptance of the group, you will become its victim. Ultimately, the factor most in your control is which group or environment you choose to become a part of. Choose a good environment, and the outcome is usually positive; choose a bad environment, and it usually won't be. It's up to you.

4.3 Over-Programming vs. The Quiet Mind

When students report that the number one reason they drink and do drugs is to reduce the stress in their lives, especially the stress caused by school, it's time to sit up and take notice. Before we deal with the stress question, though, we want to remind you again that the use of alcohol and drugs does not reduce the stress in your life. In fact, drug and alcohol use actually serves to add stress to your life. If you want to reduce stress, you're going to have to find some other way to get the job done.

A major source of stress in many young people's lives lies in the fact that they are over-scheduled. If you have an obligation to do something every minute of the day, you are a prime candidate for burnout. While it's true there are many different personality styles, and some people fare better under heavy workloads than do others, we're confident in saying that people are not built to go full force 24/7. Occasionally, you have to give yourself a break.

One of the most costly consequences of over-scheduling is that it often means you aren't getting enough sleep. If you find yourself borrowing from sleep time in order to finish your homework, you are going to suffer the consequences. Lack of a proper amount of sleep carries dire consequences for young people, and yet most of our students report getting less than seven hours of sleep per night while in high school. Not only can this have a negative impact on grades, it can increase stress, and that in turn leads to the temptation to abuse substances.

Please note: lack of sleep caused by too much video gaming or procrastination is a different animal, and yet while not directly caused by over-scheduling, it is still just as harmful. If you need help establishing priorities, please read about goal setting in section 2.3. If, however, you are burning the candle at both ends and trying to figure out if you can light the middle, you need to take a realistic look at what that is costing you.

The negative consequences of ongoing, unrelenting stress are profound—heart disease, psychiatric illnesses, cancer, and drug and alcohol abuse are but a few. Young people exposed to chronic stress may be affecting how their brains develop, and not in a good way. **Self-medicating** to deal with the symptoms of stress has become a national crisis, but it is a crisis with a treatment. We owe it to ourselves to learn how to deal with negative stress.

The first (and hardest) thing to realize about stress caused by over-scheduling is that there is a simple solution—choose to do less. That, however, flies in the face of what most of our students are about. If you want to get into a top-tier college you have to get great grades, play multiple sports, volunteer in your community, play a musical instrument, and discover the secret to cold fusion. Somewhere in there, you might want to find some space for a boyfriend or girlfriend, and we haven't even mentioned your family yet. It's really a wonder any of our students even survives high school, much less thrives there.

127

It seems almost impossible to choose to do less, but if you don't attempt to prioritize your activities and create a sane schedule for yourself, you may end up crashing and burning. This is not something we can do for you—you're going to have to decide what matters most to you. The big issue at play here is the ability to delay gratification in some areas. You have to accept the idea that you can't have everything right now all the time. If you fail to get your head around that, you will remain a victim of over-scheduling.

Please understand, we're not talking about hours and hours spent staring at your navel. You can de-stress in very little time, comparatively. A few suggestions as to how include:

→ Tai chi, yoga, massage, and meditation can help with balance, flexibility and quieting the mind. Just 15 minutes of quiet or meditation can be refreshing.

→ A quick nap in the afternoon may feel like a waste of time, but it can do wonders to recharge your drained battery.

→ Avoid technology as your bedtime approaches. Your brain needs time to prepare for sleep, and bright screens limit its ability to do so.

→ Use a sound machine to block out noises in your sleep environment that might disturb you.

→ Music has the power to calm the mind. We would never presume to tell you what music works for you, but you can probably figure out that if the beat rate of your music is triple that of your heart, it isn't going to do much to calm you.

→ Make the hard choices—cut your afterschool activities down to a reasonable level. Only you can know what that is, but engage the help of your parents and counselors if necessary.

→ Get the right amount of sleep! Current figures from the medical community for how much sleep you should be getting are at least eight hours per night, preferably nine hours for most of you. We'd bet the house most of you aren't getting anywhere near that. (Please note: it is not possible to deprive yourself of sleep all week and then catch up by sleeping all weekend. Not enough sleep each day is unhealthy, but so is sleeping all day on the weekend. One does not fix the other.)

→ Take time to eat dinner with your family. We know you feel like you don't have the time, but a close relationship with your family is less possible if you don't eat with them. Take 30 minutes for dinner—your homework will still be there when you get done.

Lessons Learned: Over-Programming vs. The Quiet Mind

Periods of down time are essential for a balanced life. Being together is an important part of being a family, and everyone shouldn't be on the go all the time. Work with your family to prioritize the obligations in your life. Put some things off until later so you can avoid burnout. Finally—**sleep, sleep, sleep!** You need at least eight hours, preferably more.

4.4 Chunk It Down

We don't know about you, but when it comes to getting a job done, Kelly is a ninja and Jonathan is a train wreck. When told to clean your room, are you the type of person who has no idea what to do first? If so, then you are a Jonathan. When assigned a long-term project or paper, do you get a stomachache? Yes? Again with the Jonathan thing.

The secret to organizational success is to stop being a Jonathan. If all you focus on is the enormity of the task, you will find yourself overwhelmed and confused. If, instead, you chunk it down into smaller, more manageable tasks, you will be well on your way to Kellyhood.

Why would a book about drug and alcohol abuse spend time on task management? Look at it this way: as we've said, one of the major reasons cited by teens for using drugs and alcohol is to reduce the stress in their lives, especially the stress caused by school. If you can learn how to reduce the level of stress you are experiencing, you will be less likely to start using drugs and alcohol in order to cope. This is a worthy exercise.

Some people seem to be naturals when it comes to organization and task management, but we think it has more to do with a combination of factors. Certainly, there are those who are genetically better suited to being organized, but unless someone takes the time to teach these gifted people some skills, many of them are doomed to long periods of trial and error before they get efficient. With proper training, though, they will be successful very quickly. On the other hand, there are those of us who, even with proper training, really need to work at it if we are ever to get the concept!

Our daughter appears to be one of the latter. If told to clean her room, she seems to experience a mental lock up—she's paralyzed by the size of the task. If you study people who suffer from severe procrastination, you will often find that they are not lazy—they just don't know where to start! We have learned that things go much smoother if we don't just tell her to clean her room but instead have her pick up ten things and put them where they belong. (Just so we're clear here—if there is a jigsaw puzzle covering the top of her table, picking up ten pieces of the puzzle does not count as ten things. The puzzle in its entirety is one thing she can count toward her goal of ten.)

If you refer to the section on setting goals (2.3), you'll see that this fits very well with how that activity progresses best. By having her pick up ten things, we have made her more efficient by being specific, making the task measurable, and

131

giving it a finish line. She knows what to do, she knows how to measure her progress, and she knows when she is finished. Because of this, she is less stressed by the idea of cleaning her room, and because she is less stressed, she is happier.

If you're the kind of kid who can't even decide what ten things to pick up, ask for help. Most parents would be thrilled to give you suggestions on where to start.

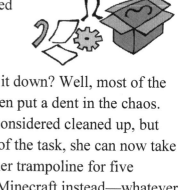

So how does this qualify as chunking it down? Well, most of the time, picking up ten things doesn't even put a dent in the chaos. More is required if the room is to be considered cleaned up, but since she has completed the first part of the task, she can now take a short break. Maybe she'll jump on her trampoline for five minutes; or she might choose to play Minecraft instead—whatever she wants to do. When the five minutes are up, though, it is time to pick up another ten things. This is the second chunk of effort she will expend. When she succeeds at that task, she gets another five-minute break.

It is the rare person indeed who can stop playing video games or some other fun activity after just five minutes. This is why you MUST incorporate the use of a timer to tell exactly when to return to the task. If you don't employ some method of knowing when to get back to work, your efforts to chunk it down are doomed. Set a timer—kitchen timer, smart phone app, whatever—and when it goes off, get back to work! No cheating! No, "I just have to save my game!" Don't be a brat—put it on pause and come back to it after the next ten things.

By doing it this way, she never gets overwhelmed by the enormity of the job. It may take her a few hours to get her room completely straightened up, but it will only feel like picking up ten things and then doing something she wants to do for a few minutes between each effort. Don't laugh—it works.

If you can't identify with the cleaning up your room example (you lucky dog—you've got staff!) you will get a better idea of what we're talking about if we use a more universal example—homework. Some of the students we work with face homework that can take hours to finish. If you start your homework each day  with feelings of depression and defeat, chunking it down can be like a lifeline thrown to someone who is drowning.

Chunking Down Homework

Let's say you have homework from four different teachers that will take you at least two hours to complete, but you're already exhausted. You can make it so much more user-friendly by just breaking it into pieces—all you need is a timer and some activity you want to pursue during your breaks. Most of you will use your phones to time your breaks, but if you go low tech, choose a timer that is accurate. If you go the low-tech route, there are some cool, cheap timers available. Our daughter uses a Donald Duck timer that you set by twisting its head. It's kind of gruesome (but also kind of cool) when you twist his head to set the time! Now that you are properly equipped, you can get started.

133

→ When you get home from school, put your backpack in its appropriate place and then wash your hands (seriously, think about what you've been touching all day! Barf!).

→ Place all your books and supplies on your desk or designated homework area.

→ Identify what has to be done. Many of you can check your assignments online, or you can refer to the homework agenda you created at school that day.

→ Establish what order you want to do your work in, and identify that order either by creating a checklist or by putting Post-its at the top of each page.

→ Now that you've organized everything, this is a good time for the first break. It's probably a good idea to have some sort of healthy snack before you get started. The last thing you need to listen to is your stomach grumbling all afternoon! Get some water, too—brains work best when they are hydrated.

→ The instant the timer rings, snack time is over and the homework begins. As we said before, the timer is the boss. When it goes off, it's time to start work—no squirreling around!

→ Finish the first of the homework tasks.

→ When you're done, put that assignment back in your pack. (So you'll have it to turn in tomorrow—there's nothing worse than doing homework and then leaving it at home. If it isn't in your hand, nobody is ever going to believe you did it!) Now go do something fun for your allotted time—play Angry Birds, do cartwheels—we don't care, just take a few minutes to relax.

→ When the timer goes off, start your second chunk of homework. Please note: rushing through the work in order to go back to playing is totally uncool. The break is a reward for doing it well, **not just doing it fast.**

→ Set the timer each time you finish a part of the homework, and continue this pattern until everything is finished. You can vary the time allotted for the breaks—if you find five minutes just isn't long enough, make it ten instead. Whatever works for you is what's most important, but is has to be short enough so you can eventually get done with this nightmare.

→ When you finally finish, don't mess up all your hard work by being disorganized at the very end. Put your homework in your backpack for the next day; and put the backpack where you can grab it and go the next morning without chaos and confusion. Guess what? You're done!

Chunking it down isn't just for cleaning rooms and homework—it works with all large tasks: household chores, yard work, etc. It will lower everyone's stress level by eliminating the battle so many kids go through with their parents over what to do, when to do it, and how it should be done. Chunk it down! Start early, and if that ship has sailed, start now! It will create a pattern of behavior that will improve the quality of your life as well as that of everyone around you. Soon, you'll find that you have time to spare.

135

Lessons Learned: Chunk it Down

 Almost every job will appear unpleasant if you look at it as a whole. By chunking it down, you downsize it and make it manageable. Quality of life is increased and stress is decreased when you break big jobs into smaller pieces.

4.5 Everybody Lies, But You Should Try Not To

Let's just get this out of the way right now—everybody lies. If you are a human and you can speak, then you have told a lie in your lifetime. That you have lied does not make you evil. It does not make you a bad person. It just means that occasionally you were less than truthful, and that is a very human trait. This does not in any way justify lying, or make it the right thing to do on all but the rarest occasions.

Why do we lie? The main reasons appear to be:
→ We don't want to be caught after doing something against the rules.
→ We don't want to suffer the consequences of said rules violations.
→ We don't want to disappoint people, especially those we value greatly, like our parents.
→ We don't want to hurt another person's feelings or cause them distress.

This is not a book meant to delve deeply into ethical debates about right and wrong—our focus is on teen substance use. The major point we want to make about lying is that it causes most people a fair amount of stress. We've discussed this numerous times in other parts of this book, but just in case you are reading out of order, we will say it again: stress is cited by most young people as the main reason they use drugs and alcohol. The fact that lying causes stress is reason enough for us to include a discussion of it here.

The first point we want to make about lying is that most of the time, it doesn't work very well. It seems like most lies are the result of the immediate impulse to avoid trouble and pain. If we have done something against the rules or someone accuses us of doing so, the first impulse for most of us is to deny it. Unfortunately, most of us don't spend a lot of time constructing seamless story lines that support our impulsive lies, and so we end up getting caught a good deal of the time.

When you are caught lying, you will often have to pay some sort of penalty for your lies. If you lie to your parents, they may punish you by taking away something you value for a time or restricting your freedom. If you are caught lying at school (and cheating is a form of lying, just so we're clear), you will probably have to suffer some sort of consequence, like a failing grade or a detention.

We want to note, though, that being caught is not the only bad thing about lying. It is that lie itself that causes a lot of the trouble. Most of the time, we will be lying to someone we know, and it is distressing to mislead a person we value. Lies are corrosive, and they cost us the comfort of good relationships with the people we are lying to. The loss of relationships is a very expensive bill to pay for an impulse.

As we said, this isn't a book on ethics, but we do want to discuss a few instances where lying and substance abuse have a wide overlap.

138

Fake ID's

Joe Fake
222 Lying Lane
Not you in the picture, CA
Not 21 & everyone knows it!

Printers today are so advanced they can create fake ID's that are almost perfect. Governments have tried to stay ahead of the counterfeit ID's by adding holograms, special inks, magnetic strips and microchips. Unfortunately, liquor stores and bars have a hard time keeping up with these innovations, and hope seems to spring eternal in the hearts of young people trying to buy booze, so fake ID's look as if they will be a part of the landscape for at least a little while longer.

If you are tempted to use one, however, please know that if you are caught, the penalties can be higher than a scolding from the clerk behind the counter or seizure of your bogus card. You can check out what penalties your state has by visiting the website for the agency that oversees alcohol distribution there, but where we live, it falls under the auspices of the California Department of Alcoholic Beverage Control.
http://www.abc.ca.gov/teencorner.html

Here's what they have to say about fake ID's:

→ *IF YOU ARE CAUGHT WITH A FAKE ID* the penalty is a minimum $250 fine and/or 24-32 hours of community service, or a maximum $1,000 fine and/or six months in the county jail, PLUS...a one year suspension of your

driver license. If you don't yet have one, you'll have to wait an extra year to get one.

→ *IF YOU ATTEMPT TO PURCHASE ALCOHOL* the penalty is a maximum $100 fine and/or 24-32 hours of community service, PLUS...a one year suspension of your driver license. If you don't yet have one, you'll have to wait an extra year to get one.

→ *IF YOU ARE CAUGHT IN POSSESSION OF ALCOHOL* the penalty is a $250 fine and 24-32 hours of community service, PLUS...a one year suspension of your driver license. If you don't yet have one, you'll have to wait an extra year to get one.

→ *IF YOU PURCHASE ALCOHOL* the fine is $250 and/or 24-32 hours of community service, PLUS...a one year suspension of your driver license. If you don't yet have one, you'll have to wait an extra year to get one.

→ ZERO TOLERANCE LAW - *IF YOU'RE UNDER 21 YEARS OLD* and have even a sip of alcohol, and you are caught driving, you'll get a 1 to 3 year suspension of your driver license.

→ *REFUSAL TO SUBMIT TO A BLOOD ALCOHOL TEST* is an admission of guilt to driving under the influence of alcohol.

Cheating on drug tests

Another area where lying and substance abuse commonly overlap is that of drug testing. We have an extensive discussion of drug testing in section 2.5, but here we are talking about efforts to get around a drug test. You don't have to be a tech wizard to know the Internet is loaded with scam artists promising you that if you just spend X amount of money you will be able to pass any drug test.

The best advice we can give you is this:

Save your money. Even if you do spend all kinds of cash on some silly kit to dodge a drug test and end up passing, in all likelihood that just means you would have passed anyway. Drug testing is an inexact science, and that's one of the reasons we don't advocate it very often. As far as we're concerned, the best way to pass a drug test is to not use drugs.

Also, if you are using drugs and you happen to pass a drug test, please don't think that you've gotten away with anything. Drug and alcohol use comes with its own set of consequences, and even though your true costs may be years down the road, you are paying today in the form of stress caused by your lying. You aren't getting away with anything, actually.

And finally:
The Biggest Lie Ever Told: "It's not mine."

Hands down—the most ridiculous and yet most frequently used dodge teens try to pull when they get caught with drugs is, "It's not mine. I'm holding it for a friend." Here is the translation of what those words actually mean: "It's mine, but I'm betting you're naïve enough and so blinded by hope and love that you'll grab any lifeline and believe this ridiculous lie."

Occasionally, this topic comes up in classes with Jonathan's older students. When he asks what the first words out of a kid's mouth are when he or she is caught with drugs, the students' response comes in the form of a chorus, "It's not mine!"

141

 Let's be clear here—kids don't ask other kids to hold drugs for them. When Jonathan was using, the last thing anyone would do was give him drugs to hold. Do that, and you were never going to see them again. Your parents weren't born yesterday, so don't disrespect them in such a ridiculous way. Tell the truth and don't further compound the consequences. In this instance, being caught may be the best thing that ever happens to you.

 ## Lessons Learned: Try Your Best Not To Lie
When you do, you compromise valuable relationships, cause yourself unnecessary stress, and compound the risk that you'll end up self-medicating your guilt with drugs and alcohol. It isn't worth it.

142

Part 5
How To Help A Friend While Keeping Yourself Safe

5.1 How To Tell If A Friend Is In Trouble

Parents are frequently confused by what constitutes a "drug problem", especially if it is their child using drugs or alcohol. They regularly tell us about kids who drink or use drugs, but then rush to point out, "But he's a really good kid," or, "She still gets great grades in school." They are worried about the fact that the child is using, but seem to want direct evidence of harm caused by that use before they intervene in the situation.

It makes us wonder: if adults and parents can't get a handle on what constitutes problem use, how are you supposed to tell whether a friend or family member is in trouble with drugs and alcohol? In this section, we're going to give you a list of signs that a friend is headed in the wrong direction.

Before we can even begin a discussion of what defines a drug or alcohol problem in the life of a teenager, we want to be very clear: current science overwhelmingly indicates that teens can't use safely. That's why we always insist that there is no level of drinking or drug use that is safe or healthy for teens.

At this point, many people attempt to dissect that statement detail by detail. The questions usually go something like, "Will a sip of beer or wine at the dinner table hurt my teen?" or "What about

143

communion wine—are you trying to tell me my child will become an alcoholic because of a religious ceremony?"

 Let's take those two questions in reverse order. We are going to go out on a limb here and state unequivocally that taking communion, in and of itself, has never—not once—caused a person to become an alcoholic. Can we back that up with proof? No, but nor do we feel the need to—it's just too silly to discuss.

Yet the first question seems almost as silly—can one sip of beer or wine from a parent's drink hurt a kid? Again, by itself, no. A sip of alcohol isn't enough of a dose to cause a teen harm. The most important thing to realize, though, is that it's not how much alcohol that sip contains that causes concern—it is what the sip represents that worries us. It represents parental permission to use alcohol. That does not doom all kids who have a sip of their dad's beer to a life of alcoholism, but it does open the door for some to explore further use under other circumstances.

In some cases, the sip at the dinner table becomes the beer at the party, the first beer makes the next one more possible, and all of a sudden, a sip has resulted in another teen starting to drink regularly. There is, in fact, evidence that says adolescents who have sipped from their parents' drinks by the age of 10 are twice as likely to have started drinking by the age of 14. When you read the section on risk factors that increase the chances a person will have drug and alcohol problems, you will see that drinking at or before 14 is a major risk.

144

That's the reason we are so comfortable when we say teens simply shouldn't use at all. While individual examples—in this case, sips of a parent's drink—may not appear to cause harm, what they frequently do cause (further use in other circumstances) is simply too great a cost for such a small act. This pattern holds true in almost every "what if" a parent throws at us concerning situations where teens consume alcohol or drugs—small, seemingly harmless behaviors become major problems when they become patterns of use, which they frequently do.

Now that we've gotten that out of the way, let's get back to the original issue—how can you tell if a friend has a problem with drugs or alcohol? The list that follows is extensive. There are dozens of signs that can indicate the presence of a problem.

Again, some of them can look small when they occur infrequently or by themselves, but when they become a part of a larger pattern, they get scary fast. As you try to apply the things on this list to a friend you are concerned about, look for patterns. If a pattern of troubling signs and behaviors starts to form, your concerns become more and more justified. It is our opinion that any teen use is harmful and unhealthy, but when assessing whether your friend has a problem, understand that the more of these signs your friend is exhibiting, the greater the chances are they need help immediately.

While this list is extensive, it is in no way all-inclusive. What you should keep in mind is that any behavior that makes you uncomfortable or causes you concern is reason enough to decide your friend may be in trouble. Remember, any use by teens is a big deal, but when these signs crop up, you should be very concerned.

Signs That a Friend May Have a Drug or Alcohol Problem:

→ Gets drunk or high on a regular basis.

→ Drinks or uses drugs when he/she is alone.

→ Drinks or gets high before, during, or after school.

→ Drinks to feel normal.

→ Lies about his/her drinking or drug use.

→ Avoids you in order to get drunk or high.

→ Takes risks, including sexual risks, when drunk or high.

→ Has frequent hangovers.

→ Has "blackouts" -- forgets what he or she did the night before while drinking.

→ Drives after drinking or getting high.

→ Constantly talks about drinking or using other drugs.

→ Avoids friends who choose not to drink or use drugs.

→ Pressures you or anyone else to drink or get high.

→ Spends more and more time with people who drink or get high.

→ Feels guilty about his/her drinking or drug use.

→ Drinks or uses more than before in order to feel drunk or high.

→ Thinks it's hard to have a good time if not drinking or getting high.

→ Borrows or steals money to buy drugs or alcohol.

→ Makes the decision not to drink or use drugs and then fails to follow through.

→ Lies about how much alcohol or other drugs he or she is using.

→ Loses interest in things that used to mean a lot, like schoolwork, sports, hobbies, or friends who don't drink or use drugs.

→ Parents, teachers, co-workers, or friends have told him/her to stop drinking or using drugs.

→ Plans drinking or drug use in advance.

→ Needs drugs or alcohol to cope with everyday life.

146

→ Has broken plans with you, or showed up late, because he/she was getting drunk or high.

→ Shows up at school drunk or high or has skipped class to use.

→ Gets in trouble with the police or other authority figures.

→ Drinks to steady his/her nerves or to get rid of a hangover.

→ Has had a frightening experience with drugs or alcohol but continues to use.

→ Gets annoyed when people criticize his/her drinking.

→ Drinks or uses drugs in places or situations that you would rather avoid.

→ Uses drugs or alcohol to avoid painful feelings.

→ Feels run-down, hopeless, depressed, or even suicidal as a result of drinking or drug use.

5.2 What If It's Bigger Than You Can Handle?

Alright, first things first—if your friend is in trouble with drugs or alcohol, it's already bigger than you can handle. You can get all offended if you want to, but (and you can do this in a Doctor Phil voice in your head if necessary) you need to listen up—you do not have the resources or the experience required to give your friend the help they need. In fact, if you are keeping their secret and trying to help them by yourself, you are actively keeping them from getting the help they need. You are hurting your friend with your version of help. We know that stings, but it's true.

To us, all teen drug and alcohol use is unacceptable. Some teen use, though, gets to the point where immediate harm or death is possible. In cases such as this, your friend needs the services of an assessment professional—someone who can determine the depth and extent of the use that now exists. Depending on what the assessment shows, they may recommend drug treatment or a support program so your friend can stop using. In order for this to happen, you need the help of an adult, and you have to make the painful decision to tell someone what's going on.

We hope that that person will be one of your parents, but in cases where that isn't possible, you may have to turn a counselor at school, a member of your religious community, your family doctor, or some other adult you trust that is in a position to help. The bottom line, though, is you have to tell an adult.

We understand how hard it is to tell on someone. It goes against almost everything we've been told—mind your own business, nobody likes a tattle tale, don't be a snitch. Unfortunately, none of

148

that matters in this case. Your friend is in trouble, and you may be the only person with the courage to get the help needed.

Obviously, this is a worst-case scenario, but one thing we've learned over the years is that drugs and alcohol have the potential to take the best people to the darkest places. It doesn't happen to everyone, it doesn't even happen to most, but everyone it happens to has one thing in common—no one ever thought it would come to that. When it does, you have to act; you can't just sit around hoping it will get better.

We don't want to kid you here—this will not be pretty. At first, your friend will probably be so angry they won't speak to you anymore. That's ok. Once they have stopped using for a while, they may come to understand what it is you have done, and they might even thank you for saving them.

Even if that never happens though, you have to understand that what you did was critically necessary. Sometimes, and especially in cases where drugs and alcohol are the problem, you have to be willing to give up the friendship in order to save the friend. It is an act of maturity and character, and as you probably already know, when those two words appear in close proximity, there's going to be some pain involved. No joke—you did good work, it just feels bad at first.

PS—If you're completely stuck and don't know where to turn, we have help and referral information on our website at: www.milestogodrugedcation.com.

5.3 How to Assess a Party

You would be totally justified in thinking (since this is a book about helping teens avoid drug and alcohol use) that we are going to be feverishly anti-party. Justified, yes—and completely wrong. Let's be clear—we think teen parties are incredibly important and valuable. The average teen party provides almost infinite opportunities for you to develop social skills, manage risk, resist impulse, test boundaries, and fine-tune your sense of responsibility. (Oh yeah—occasionally you'll have a really good time, too!) If you never get a chance to practice these skills, you are very unlikely possess them as an adult.

Unfortunately, the majority of teen parties also feature the use of alcohol and other drugs, and that's where they transition from valuable social petri dishes to dangerous, potentially deadly nightmares of excess. The point where drugs and alcohol make their entrance at parties is the same point where we withdraw our support for them.

The presence of drugs and alcohol is why your parents often wish you could gain these skills some other way, at some place other than a party. You can, but it isn't easy. In our presentations, we often ask parents,

If the stated goal is to have a good time with large numbers of their peers, what options are available to teens other than parties?

Certainly, other opportunities exist, but they are harder to come by. When compared to the ease of finding out about and attending your average party, a large-scale trip to Disneyland with 50 or 60 of your closest friends seems to require the complex planning of a trip to Mars!

Until we come up with better alternatives, then, parties appear to be the best option for teens who want to socialize in large groups. If that's the case, you're going to have to figure out how to assess what's going on at each respective party before plunging headlong into them. The last thing we want is for you to end up in the middle of an out-of-control riot without an exit strategy.

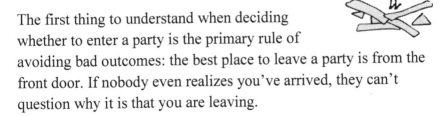

The first thing to understand when deciding whether to enter a party is the primary rule of avoiding bad outcomes: the best place to leave a party is from the front door. If nobody even realizes you've arrived, they can't question why it is that you are leaving.

Imagine that you've entered a party without any forethought—you just wade into the middle of the room and start looking around to see who's there. Almost immediately, you catch the eye of a friend, and that person grabs you by the arm and says in a way-too-loud voice,

In just a few minutes, though, you realize that almost everyone in the room is completely hammered—some of them are drunk out of their minds! Can you, in this circumstance, grab your coat and head for the door, or are you kind of stuck? If you try to leave, the first questions you'll have to answer are:

(Our daughter is lucky in this regard—can you imagine a better excuse when somebody passes you a beer than, "Seriously? My parents are the Drug Guys.")

But what are you supposed to say? Something like, "This party is a threat to my personal safety!" isn't going to do much to elevate your social status in the eyes of your friends; and excuses like, "My parents would be really upset if they knew I was here" won't win you a lot of street cred either.

While it's certainly true your parents would be upset (and to us that makes it a very valid reason for not wanting to be there), some people are going to find that a pretty lame excuse for leaving a party. So what do you do?

→ Are you just supposed to accept defeat and get used to the idea that you're trapped for the time being?

→ Do you leave, and pay the price of lost social status in order to keep your parents happy?

Tough questions, right?

Yes, they are, so let's table them for now and explore the idea that there is a way to avoid the whole mess in the first place.

 Remember—the easiest place to leave a party is from the front door. The question now, though, is how can you tell which parties to enter and which ones to avoid?

The skill required here is called "**reading a room**", and it is one of the most important tools you can have as you attempt to survive

your teen years. Once you learn to recognize the signs, you are going to be able to tell, in about 60 seconds, how drunk the people in the room are.

That information will then allow you to decide if you want to be a part of what's going on, and if the answer is no, allow you to leave before anyone even sees that you've arrived.

154

You've probably noticed that we said this skill would allow you to tell how drunk people are, and that seems to indicate that alcohol is the only drug you need to worry about. Realistically speaking, you are going to face other challenges than just alcohol as you navigate the party scene, but as we've noted in other sections of this book, alcohol is the most frequently used drug by teens.

Other drugs are certainly cause for concern, but alcohol is the 900-pound gorilla of teen use. For that reason, we are primarily going to discuss how to deal with alcohol. If you can master this skill, the majority of the work is already done.

So, how do you read a room?

The first thing to remember is that drunk people actually give off signs that indicate where they are on a scale that goes from sober, through mild intoxication, then to absolutely slaughtered, and finally ends in death.

Wait a minute! Death? Does that mean that every time your parents have wine with dinner you have to be freaking out about whether they are going to die? Of course it doesn't. In order to get that far down the scale a person has to behave in a very irresponsible way, and that isn't the way most people behave when they have wine with dinner.

On the other hand, your friends can end up in desperate trouble faster than you imagine if they drink too much too quickly. So we appear to be saying that adults can drink safely and moderately but teenagers can end up at great risk by doing almost the same thing—that's just confusing! We know. If, however, you work with this assumption — that it is not possible for teens to use alcohol in a safe or healthy way, despite the fact that some adults can—you can lessen the confusion somewhat. If you are looking at a drinking teen, you are looking at a problem in the making.

As we said earlier, if you want to be able to read a room you'll need to be able to recognize drunk people quickly, and in order to do that you need to know what to look for.

When we discuss the stages of intoxication, we describe drunk people in six stages:

1. They get loud.
2. Their motor skills deteriorate.
3. Their senses deteriorate.
4. They pass out.
5. They lapse into a coma.
6. They die.

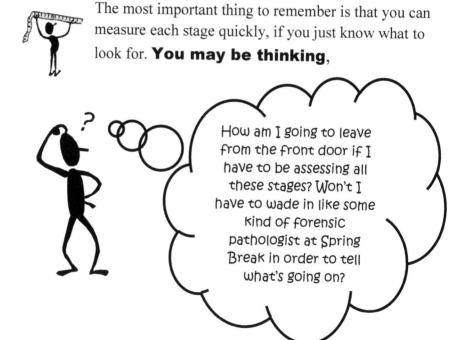

The most important thing to remember is that you can measure each stage quickly, if you just know what to look for. **You may be thinking,**

How am I going to leave from the front door if I have to be assessing all these stages? Won't I have to wade in like some kind of forensic pathologist at Spring Break in order to tell what's going on?

Not really. Now, admittedly, we have slightly over-simplified things—you aren't going to be able to see every sign every time—but please believe us when we tell you that you will almost always be able to assess intoxication, and you will be able to do it quickly. Stay calm—we'll get you there.

The other thing to keep in mind is these stages can be assessed in people you don't know—you don't need a baseline behavior off of which you measure variations.

Ok, let's look at each stage in detail, so you'll know exactly what to look for as you enter a party.

Stage 1: They get loud.

Have your parents ever invited a bunch of friends over to the house for drinks? If they have, one thing you will notice is that the amount of alcohol served is directly proportional to the noise level in the room. In other words, the more the guests drink, the more noise they make. Admittedly, sober parties are noisy, but drunk parties are just ridiculous! Once you hear drunk loud, you'll instantly recognize it each subsequent time you hear it after that.

Why do drunk people get so loud? There are a number of reasons, the most powerful of which is that alcohol consumption almost immediately results in decreased inhibition. What that means is that one of the first things alcohol takes away is your ability to behave the way you normally do. This loss of control can show up in many different ways—increased aggression, ill-advised romantic activity, increased use of inappropriate language (profanity), ignorance of personal space boundaries—but one of

157

the quickest and most notable is the inability to modulate the volume of your voice.

One other factor may be that alcohol is a **central nervous system (CNS) depressant**—in other words, it slows down or stops the transmission of nervous messages carried by the spinal cord and the brain. Since hearing is almost purely a CNS function, it makes sense that, as a person gets more intoxicated, they will be less aware of or bothered by loud noise. As a result, parties that feature alcohol use will unfailingly be louder affairs than are those without alcohol.

So, how can you assess intoxication at a party that is currently at Stage 1 drunkenness? First, take a quick look around to check for the presence of alcohol—is there a keg, a bar, or hundreds of red plastic cups? If so, you can assume alcohol is present. That does not, however, prove that intoxication is present. For that, you will use the level of noise—the louder it is, the drunker it is.

Stage 2: Their motor skills deteriorate.

In case you're not clear: motor skills are the ability to make your body move in response to messages from your brain. Motor skills are critically important in areas like driving and sports, but they can be important in much more mundane ways, such as in the actions of standing, walking, and speaking. When people consume alcohol, all these activities are negatively affected. You should note that we are not talking about the puke-spewing, staggering dervish normally associated with excess drinking—that comes later. This is a much more subtle effect, and because it's more subtle it will be a little harder for you to see, unless you know what to look for.

The first thing to realize is that we dramatically underestimate how complex the activity of standing on two feet is. Most people aren't consciously aware that when we are standing still we are not actually still—when we stand we actually sway forward and backward in a pattern. Normally, we have very little difficulty doing this without any conscious thought, and the sway is  microscopically subtle. When a person gets drunk, though, they aren't able to keep up with the swaying pattern. Remember, the messages relayed to the brain when alcohol is present in our blood are delivered more slowly—in other words, they arrive in the brain later than they should.

It's pretty easy to imagine where this ends up—the sway becomes more pronounced, and occasionally we have to perform what we call a gross body posture correction. That means we have to do something big to keep from falling over, like grab onto a nearby object or move one of our feet to prevent toppling over. Admittedly, stage one is easier to assess quickly—just check for alcohol and listen to the noise level in the room, and you have it. Judging the intensity of sway is a lot more difficult, but diagnosing intoxication is easier if we combine the inability to stand normally with the other two areas we listed—walking and speaking.

You don't have to watch too many episodes of "Cops" to know that drunk people are really bad at walking. The lack of coordination caused by alcohol powerfully affects the ability to walk, especially if you want to walk in a straight line. Granted, people at parties don't generally mill around like schools of fish, so you may not instantly be able to assess walking ability every time, but you can use it when you see it.

The final thing to check is how clearly people are speaking. If you've ever heard drunk people talk, it is almost immediately apparent that they don't do it well—the classic slurring of words, the increase in volume of speech, and the lack of coherent thought can all combine to help you assess Stage 2 intoxication. If it is at all possible, when you first arrive at a party, take a moment or two to watch and listen to the crowd. Are they having trouble standing, walking, or speaking? If so, you are witnessing Stage 2 intoxication.

Stage 3: Their senses deteriorate.

In Stage 3 intoxication, drinkers lose their senses—their ability to judge hot, cold, and pain. This does not mean they lose their common sense—they lost that back in Stage 1. If you take a moment to remember what central nervous system depressant do, you realize that very drunk people are seriously compromised in their ability to transmit  important information from their bodies to their brains. In Stage 3, information that typically serves to warn you that you are being injured no longer makes it to your brain quickly enough for you to react in time.

If a person is Stage 3 drunk, by the time their brain feels the pain the injury has already occurred. Pain, while certainly unpleasant, serves to warn us. It tells us to move away from the cause of the pain, and thereby stop the injury from worsening. Alcohol in doses large enough to cause Stage 3 intoxication can stop pain almost entirely, and injuries received in this stage can be severe as a result. Your body just never tells your brain to move away from the threat!

Alcohol really does have a big effect on how we feel pain. In the days before effective general anesthesia, alcohol was sometimes used to dull the senses so the patient couldn't feel the pain of  surgery. Unfortunately, doses large enough to be effective also caused nausea, loss of consciousness, and death. You can take two things from that—alcohol is a terrible anesthetic, and if you are drunk enough to not feel pain effectively, you are drunk enough to start worrying about nausea, loss of consciousness, and death. Of course, you'll also be so drunk it won't even occur to you to worry, and that's a big part of the problem—when you get this drunk, you really stink at self-protection.

So how are you supposed to tell if party-goers have lost the ability to feel hot, cold and pain? Most people have never had the thought, "Hmmmm. Now where did I put my branding iron?" Very few have considered bringing a fistful of darts to a party for the purpose of some long-distance pain inspiration. In fact, it's quite difficult to name a socially acceptable or legal way to test for pain in a party setting, so that really isn't a very good way for you to judge intoxication in this stage.

So, how do you do it, then? Actually, in order to judge Stage 3 drunk, all you have to do is remember from our list what Stage 4 is: **They pass out.** Trust us when we say that if your friend is in Stage 3 intoxication, you will be afraid for their safety. They are literally knocking on the door of losing consciousness, which means they are so drunk as to be frightening. You don't really need a skill to see if someone is this drunk. They will either be behaving so outrageously that you will wonder if it is still the same person you knew just a few hours ago (in the good old days, when he or she was sober) or they will be almost totally checked out mentally. They are going to be having great difficulty standing and walking, and their speech will be nearly or totally impossible to understand. At this point, if you care about them at all, you will be deeply concerned. You should be, especially if they have consumed enough to reach the next stage.

Stage 4: They pass out.

If it ever gets to the point where a friend loses consciousness from drinking, many teens think that since the person is no longer able to drink (you know, because their arms and legs no longer work—that makes it pretty hard to drink anymore) that they are no longer at risk. These people seem to think that the loss of consciousness is some sort of safety valve!

Unfortunately, that is not the case. In fact, it is just the opposite. It is not well known that teens are, generally speaking, more resistant to the effects of alcohol than adults are. Now before you

162

go getting all proud of yourself, you should know that this isn't a positive thing. If drinking teens actually do lose consciousness, it means they have been drinking rapidly, aggressively, and in great quantity relative to their body size.

This aggressive, rapid drinking style also means that these teens frequently have a backlog of drinks in their stomachs and small intestines that has yet to be absorbed into their bloodstreams. When teens lose consciousness due to alcohol, often they will keep getting drunker for two to three hours more as these surplus drinks are absorbed. Unfortunately, this happens despite the fact that they are no longer actively consuming alcohol. This can be fatally misleading: they are no longer drinking, but they are still getting drunker, which means they may possibly transition into **Stages 5 and 6: coma and death.**

How are you supposed to tell if your friend is unconscious and not just sleeping?

Well, the first thing you have to realize is that you aren't going to get this done from the front door. Your days of flying under the radar are over. If you arrive at a party and find that one of your friends is so drunk they may be unconscious, you will be forced to make a choice—ignore them and hope for the best (NOT the right choice) or get them help if they need it.

You'll be able to tell if they are desperately in trouble if they can no longer respond to pain, and the time for joking about branding irons and darts is over. You need to know if their brain is still

163

active, and the inability to respond to pain is a powerful indication that it is not. Luckily, there is a relatively safe, quick pain test known as a sternum rub. To perform one, you just place one or two of your knuckles on the bony plate in the middle of the person's chest (the sternum), press down with moderate pressure and rub in quick, tight circles.

Be very aware: this isn't funny, and you can injure someone seriously if you start messing around. There is no need to put your body weight into the effort—just press and rub. All you have to do to see why this works is to try it on yourself. You'll quickly find out it REALLY HURTS!

We are so serious about this next section that we are inserting a medical liability disclaimer here to emphasize our point!

__Medical Liability Disclaimer:__ The information contained in this book is meant to provide the reader with information for drug abuse prevention purposes only. It is not a substitute for medical advice, diagnosis or treatment. A medical professional should be contacted immediately in cases of substance abuse and possible overdose. ALWAYS CALL 911 in the event of an emergency. The publisher and author are not responsible for any specific health or allergy needs that may require medical supervision and are not liable for any damages, injury, hospitalization, coma, death or negative consequences from any treatment, action, application or preparation, to any person reading or following the information in this book. References are provided for informational purposes only and do not constitute endorsement of any treatment, websites or other sources. While the authors have made every effort to provide accurate information and internet addresses at the time of publication, neither the publisher nor the authors assume any responsibility for errors or changes that occur after publication.

If your friend doesn't scream in pain when you do a sternum rub, they really are in danger. **The next thing you need to do is call**  **911.** One more time for clarity—if your friend is unconscious from drinking, they need medical attention! **Call 911,** no matter what everyone else tells you. When the person at the other end answers with, **"911, what is your emergency?"** you need to say, **"My friend has been drinking. They have lost consciousness and are no longer responding to pain cues. Please send an ambulance."** While you wait for the ambulance to arrive, you should *place your friend on their side* and make sure they are still breathing. If they start to puke, which is quite likely, you want to make sure they don't choke on their vomit. The best way to do this is to *place their cheek on their outstretched arm* so that the vomit will leak out of their mouth and not back down their throat. Yes, it's disgusting, but it is also necessary if you want your friend to survive until the ambulance arrives. By the way: are you having fun yet? Probably not. But wait—it gets worse.

Stage 5: They lapse into a coma.

A coma is a profound state of unconsciousness. The person won't respond to any external stimuli, including light, pain, or sound. It will be impossible for you to tell what level of unconsciousness or coma your friend is in, but at this point, they may experience a lack of oxygen that has the potential to lead to brain damage and death. If you haven't figured this out by now, we want you to know that the situation is beyond your ability to manage at this point—in fact, is has been for a while.

165

Despite what anyone says, your friend needs professional help, and if you don't get it for them, they may die. It may not be clear to you yet, but you'll soon figure out that while calling an ambulance sounds like a good idea as you read this, in a party environment it won't be so easy. If you announce to the party that you are about to call 911, you should get ready to be abused. It's not that you are going to suffer physical abuse, although you may. It's more likely that a number of other teens will actively try to talk you out of doing so. They will try to convince you that passing out is normal—they see it all the time and nothing bad ever happens!

The problem is, what they say often appears to be true. Not every teen who passes out ends up in a coma—in fact, not many do. Your difficulty is:

YOU CAN'T TELL THE DIFFERENCE BETWEEN PASSED OUT AND COMA.

You may not even be able to tell if your friend is dead or alive for critical moments when a call to 911 might still save them. If you bow to the pressure here and fail to make the 911 call, you may regret it for the rest of your life.

As you can see, this is brutally hard to figure out. Your friend might be asleep, they might be passed out, they might be in a coma—you can't tell. They might need an ambulance, they might recover on their own—you can't tell. If you call 911, the party will not survive the visit by the police and the ambulance—that's a fact. Your actions will not be popular with your peers—that's another fact. What started as an attempt to socialize and have fun is now wildly complicated and frightening. Unfortunately, there is one last stage.

166

Stage 6: They die.

While tens of thousands of people die each year in the U.S. due to the use of alcohol, it is nearly impossible to find any reliable statistics for how many actually die as a direct result of alcohol overdose. As far as we can tell, fewer than 2,000 of these tens of thousands of deaths are directly the result of alcohol overdose. Two thousand—that doesn't sound like many. Think about it— almost 500,000 people die each year in the U.S. because of tobacco use. That's a half million people. Two thousand seems like a drop in the bucket—until one of those 2,000 is a friend of yours. Then it seems like a lot of people.

Add to that the fact that many of these people die because of conscious inaction on the part of friends and peers at parties. It's our opinion that at least a few of them may have survived if someone just called 911 sooner, but they chose not to because they didn't want to get in trouble, or they didn't want to lose social status by being a snitch. If you're the person who chooses to not make the call, there will be lot of guilt and "what ifs" in your life from now on.

 If you don't think this party sounds like a lot of fun anymore, you're right. **How can you avoid all this turmoil and confusion?**

Learn how to read the room.

We know, it's not as easy as it sounded in the beginning—we get that. But you need to start thinking about what your definition of fun is.

Help me out here—am I having fun yet?

If you enter a party and can see the signs of Stage 1 and Stage 2 intoxication, can you see any way the party is going to end up getting more sober rather than more intoxicated? What do you think is going to happen if you choose to enter and stay? It's your choice—you just have to realize what your choice may end up putting you in the middle of.

A lot of teens we talk to say they can't actually remember how they ended up going to these kinds of parties. If you were to sit in on any of our classes with younger students (many just like you) you would find that most of them know they don't belong at parties where teens are using alcohol or drugs. It's just wrong, and they know it. They also know their parents would be losing it if they caught their kid at one of these parties.

If you were to wait a few years, though, and check back with the same groups of kids, you would find that many of them are now at these parties on a regular basis.

How does this happen?

When did they decide it would be ok to put themselves in this type of risk-filled environment?

The answer is usually that it isn't one big decision that puts them there—it's a bunch of small ones, made over a number of years. Remember, too, that a lot of what ends up happening depends upon what friends you choose to spend time with. If you hang around with a bunch of party kids, chances are very good you will end up being one too. If instead you choose to spend your free time with kids who don't drink and use, you probably won't end up doing it either.

168

It seems to boil down to how you view the two different groups. A lot of kids we talk to seem to end up thinking that the people who go to parties are the popular, cool group—the group lots of people want to be a part of.

On the other hand, many see the non-using group as less popular—as losers. To us, that's a broken definition. Unfortunately, we don't get to make the choice of who you hang out with—you have to make that choice. It's one of the most important choices people make, and yet many times it seems people don't put a lot of thought into it. They want to be popular and accepted, and the party people seem to be the ones defined by the group as the popular people, so that's where you should go, right? Maybe not.

If, instead, you think the kids who get their joy from being in a theater group, or playing a musical instrument, or pursuing any passion other than partying are the cool ones, you have a better chance of not spending your entire teenage life chasing the party.

We hope so, because parties that feature the use of drugs and alcohol are way more complicated and a lot less fun than they first appear.

Lessons Learned:
Please, Learn How To Read A Room

And if you happen to find a party where a bunch of really nice people have gotten together to have a good time without drinking and doing drugs—have a good time! That, after all, is what parties are supposed to be about. Enjoy!

169

Part 6
How We Became The Drug Guys

6.1 Jonathan's Story: I was born in the middle of the 1950's. My family was what many people at the time would have called typical: my dad was an officer in the Navy, and my mother, despite the fact that she was a college graduate and a registered nurse, was a stay-at-home mom most of the time.

When we were young, our family went on vacation each year to this idyllic campground on the shores of Long Lake in Maine. On the way, we spent lots of time with extended family, and we regularly saw cousins, aunts, uncles and grandparents. I think that out of 1,000 people, 999 of them would have come out of the experience happy, healthy, and well adjusted. I didn't.

One problem for me was how often we had to move to a new home. Because of my dad's military service, we moved almost a dozen times when I was young. That meant always being the new kid in class, a role I despised. My dad was also a submariner, and that required that he be away from home for half of each year—he was home for three months, then he'd be gone for the next three. This meant my mom was regularly left to raise five children by herself.

My mom was funny, artistic and caring, but she was a victim of her time—a lot of military wives of the day did as they were told, kept their complaints to themselves, took diet pills to look good, took sleeping pills to counter the diet pills, and drank to deal with the isolation and pressure of single parenthood. In her later years, my mom's drinking became more of an issue. We didn't appreciate it at the time, but problems with alcohol had plagued her family for generations.

The first emotion I remember feeling was fear, and that was followed closely by loneliness. I was terrified to be left alone, and I remember being so afraid that I would feel physically ill on the way to a new school or summer camp. My relationships were fleeting, my role models were inadequate or absent, and my heart was broken. My dad was a tough disciplinarian, and my older brother became a troubled bully of a kid.

In light of all this, my first drug experience seems a foregone conclusion. I was in third grade, the new kid in class, and desperate to be liked and accepted by the cool kids. As it happened, the coolest kid in our third grade class at the time was this boy named Clifford.

One day after school, Clifford said to me, "We're going over to my house to smoke cigarettes—you want to come?" In about a second, I did all the calculations. If I got caught, my parents would be livid and the punishment would be mighty. Saying no would make me a baby in the eyes of the boys I was so desperate to impress. Saying yes would tell them I was one of Clifford's smoking gang, and I'd gain the status associated with that position. To me, this was a no-brainer—I was going to smoke cigarettes in Clifford's garage.

My memories of my first cigarette are still clear—it was horrific. The smoke burned my throat, sinuses, and lungs. My eyes watered, I was so dizzy I thought I would fall down, and my stomach was doing flip-flops. My hands shook and I was pouring sweat. The taste in my mouth was so awful all I wanted to do was spit, but we were in Clifford's garage, so I just kept swallowing the nauseating saliva I was producing in such vast quantities. In all, it was the worst thing I had ever purposely done to myself, and yet in my eyes it was so worth it. I got to be a part of something I so desperately wanted—these guys acted like I was their friend.

Smoking, as nasty as it was, made me a part of a peer group. Smoking socialized me when nothing in my almost nonexistent skill set did. To me, it felt like smoking fixed me.

The next couple of drugs I used, alcohol and marijuana, followed pretty much the same pattern. I drank alcohol for the first time at the age of 12 in an effort to win the favor of a kid named Mike, and I smoked weed for the first time at 14 so my brother and his friends wouldn't tease me when I refused. The beginnings of my substance abuse were all related to being accepted by others—the desire to not be alone.

While the reasons I started using alcohol and marijuana were similar to the ones that started my tobacco use, these drugs were more powerful—they had the ability to change how I felt. Drunk to me wasn't stupor, it was exhilarating and liberating. I felt light and free and, for the first time in my life, I wasn't afraid of everyone around me. The idea of asking a girl to dance didn't inspire terror when I was drunk; in fact, it didn't scare me at all. Smoking weed was different from being drunk, but it did the same thing—it made me not feel, and that's what I wanted.

Drug use became the default setting for me when I socialized—if I was with friends, I was always trying to construct a setting in which drug use was possible. I chose friends who would use with me so my doubts about the rightness of using were less troubling. Even when I did find friends that wanted to use, almost none of them wanted to use the way I did. My desire for drugs was

172

limitless—at the end of a binge, when everyone else just wanted to stop for the day and crawl home, I just couldn't seem to turn it off. The only thing that ever stopped my use was money. Eventually, my cash would run out and my credit would dry up, and I'd temporarily have to stop simply because I had run out of options.

After a while, I found myself much more interested in getting high than I was in anything else. I was doing a terrible job at work. I constantly lied to people about where I was and what I was doing. I either lied so I could dodge work and get high, or lied so I could dodge work and stay in bed for a few days trying to recover from a binge. When I was conscious enough to have feelings, I was wracked with guilt and self-loathing, and like any good addict, when those feelings bubbled to the surface I just nuked them out of existence with further, heavier drug use.

Eventually, my bosses grew tired of my antics, so they called me in and confronted me. They didn't know exactly what was causing my shoddy performance, but they issued an ultimatum—fix it or you're fired. Incapable of telling the truth by then, I blamed my behavior on excessive stress caused by the job.

My bosses were good people, and they offered me an out—go see the company psychologist and get some help. When I went to my first meeting with her, we hadn't been talking for more than 10 minutes when she put down her pen and said, "OK. That's enough." Confused, I asked her what she meant. She said, "Here's all you need to know. You're a drug addict and an alcoholic, and you're going to die if you don't check into treatment." When I tried to dodge and manipulate, she rephrased her initial comments with, "You're a dead man. You're just not smart enough to fall over yet."

173

I was lucky enough to work for a company that at the time was willing to pay for a 28-day inpatient drug treatment, and I was doubly lucky to be admitted to McLean's Hospital in Belmont, MA, one of the best drug rehabs in the country. They taught me what I needed to know in order to stay alive.

For the first time since I was eight, I wasn't doing drugs. It was truly amazing not to want to die every morning when I opened my eyes. It was incredible to not have every word that came out of my mouth be a lie. I no longer had to spend each morning wondering if I was going to puke my guts out in a fit of hangover-induced nausea. Yet, for all the initial relief, there was a long, painful recovery effort ahead.

Then and Now—Over Two Decades Later: When I think about the differences between what I was like as a person when I was using addictively and what I am like now as a non-user in recovery, I am most likely to think about my relationships. Family relationships are the most powerful and influential, and family includes first the people you come from and then later the people you join with and create.

When I was using, the only relationship I had that mattered was the one I had with whatever drug I had gotten my hands on. I was willing to sacrifice any personal relationships I had in order to get the drug, and that meant family, friends, loved ones—all were considered expendable when it came to using. There are a thousand different reasons why it ended up this way, but suffice it to say for our purposes here that I felt terrible about myself almost constantly. The only time I didn't feel that way was when I was high, and I never wanted to feel that way, so I tried to stay high all the time.

Of course, if you know anything about drug use on this level you know that emotions can't be effectively fixed by using. Tolerance kicks in, money problems become omnipresent, good relationships turn bad and sick relationships become downright destructive. All this leads to feeling worse than ever, and if you're like I was and drug use is your only coping skill, it soon turns into an ever increasing spiral of use followed by feeling bad followed by more use and on and on and on.

The biggest difference between then and now is how I choose to act when I feel emotions. I'm probably never going to be the poster child for high EQ, but I have picked up a few of the basics. I know that I can't change anyone but myself. I know that doing the right thing will not necessarily be rewarded by life immediately changing for the better. I know that being loved is more likely to happen to someone who has the capacity to love. I know that when I feel frustrated, angry outbursts and hurtful comments don't result in a reduction of that frustration but always make me feel guilty afterward. I know that feeling good is not the first step in the process, but the result of a continued striving to be good.

Most importantly, though, is the difference in how I treat my relationships today as opposed to when I was using. When I was using, I simply could not put anyone else first, ever. Granted, today I'm not necessarily that much better, but at least it is in my head that I should try. If someone else cooks, I should clean up. If something is important to my wife or daughter, then I should support that even if its value is not immediately apparent to me.

Ultimately, the people we become is determined by the interaction of genetics and environment. My genetics are what they are, but my emotional environment as a child and young man was an

175

awful, hurtful place. I now understand that I have the power to change the environment in which I live. My daughter will never suffer the abuse I did, and she will know every day that she is valued and loved—because I will tell her. Who she becomes is certainly not just in my hands, but largely the environment in which she grows up is, and that is the biggest difference between me then and me now. Today, there is nothing more important to me than my wife and daughter, and that, amazingly, is a place I have found I can be happy.

<u>6.2 Kelly's Story</u>: I am a drug addict magnet. I am the spouse, friend, family member and colleague of many alcoholics and drug addicts. Not just a few—a lot! My awareness of addiction began when I was in elementary school, but my understanding of it came when I was a teenager. Because I have so many people in my life who are in recovery, I must respect their anonymity. For that reason, I will not be describing my life the way that a recovering alcoholic/addict would do in an autobiography, but I can tell you about how it affected me.

When I was 19, I decided to get my Ph.D. and work with friends and family members of addicts. After having several people in my life who were forever changed by their addiction, I realized that my life was changed by the experience as well. From my perspective, when they needed help, I was the one who cleaned up the mess. I was the one who picked people up when they fell down, held people's hair while they vomited, comforted them and listened to endless babble about their life problems. They all seem to find me eventually. I got to the point where I just wanted to hide.

After a couple of years of college psychology classes, I started realizing that I was a big part of the problem. Attending Al-Anon and Alateen meetings helped explain the impact that these people and their behaviors were having on my life. While I wasn't an addict myself, I was willing to try several drugs and unfortunately liked several of them. Alcohol was not for me, I had a very low tolerance for drinking. It made me sick and I hated that out of control, sleepy feeling.

Nevertheless, since drugs and alcohol were such a prevalent part of the culture in the 70's and 80's, it was easy to copy my friends' behaviors when they started using drugs. Since I had no drug education at all, what I now see as common sense non-use decisions were not so clear to me back then. As a sickly kid and only child, I craved attention from my peers. I am the perfect example of the naïve lamb heading for the slaughter. These are the kids I watch for today that I label the "followers."

Each person experiences drugs in their own way, and some drugs were more attractive to me than others were. I have dyslexia and ADHD, but at that time, I was still undiagnosed. I am so hyperactive (or "naturally caffeinated" as I tell my students) that I found myself attracted to prescription and over the counter drugs that would give me clarity and focus or help me sleep at night. I also regularly sought relief, via the use of prescription and OTC drugs, from the pain of a previous back injury. I was self-medicating, but it wasn't until much later that I learned what that meant. Fortunately, I was the type of person that was able to say, "I don't like what this is doing to my life," and so I stopped before it got completely out of control. My common sense finally kicked in.

In the early 80's, I watched as more and more people around me destroyed themselves with drugs and alcohol, and by the time I was 22 years old I had witnessed several suicide attempts by people close to me. I got scared and decided to abstain from

177

alcohol entirely, which I did for years. Finally, after a few years of school, I realized that I had no desire to spend the rest of my working life listening to people's problems as a psychologist.

At that point, I changed course, went to film/theater school, and fell in love with comedy. I had always been a big fan of Bill Cosby and Bob Newhart, and I thought their jobs looked like a lot more fun than my original career track. I guess the joke was kind of on me when Newhart went on to do such brilliant comedy as a psychologist in "The Bob Newhart Show." I spent the next 10 years working in television, theater and comedy clubs. In the early 90's, I was rushing madly from film school at UCLA to the set of Full House at Sony Studios to the Groundlings on Melrose to the Laff Stop in Newport Beach.

I loved it, and met dozens of goal oriented, focused people who were following their passion, but it struck me as odd that a disproportionate number of the performers were smokers, alcoholics, and addicts. It seemed like most of the funniest performers were cast from the same mold—depressed, self-deprecating, observational comics with very real alcohol and drug habits. This is when my eyes were really opened about the level of depression and addiction that enveloped the performers. However, it wasn't just the performers—the writers were self-loathing and frustrated that their talents were not being rewarded with fame and opportunity, and the aspiring directors and producers seemed convinced they had to play the party scene to make deals. I was constantly dealing with drunks and smokers; not just on the stage, but in the audience as well. I was annoyed and frustrated.

Then, in January of 1992, I lost my home, my pets and all of my belongings in a fire caused by a faulty extension cord. Haunted by loss and heartbreak, I decided to leave California and take a job at a comedy club in Harvard Square in Cambridge. After a year of being in the coldest place I'd ever been in my life, a friend of mine said that she knew a comic that I should meet, because she thought we would have a lot in common. I had just opened my own comedy club, and was attempting to do something special with one-person shows. My first response was "NO, I don't date the comics!" It was the cardinal rule that Cindy Stewart, my good friend and longtime manager of another comedy club taught me— don't date the talent! My friend finally wore me down and convinced me I should give this guy a chance. When I first saw Jonathan, my immediate thought was that he was too tall for me (I'm 5'1" and he's 6'2"), but I spoke with him briefly. We eventually met again at an event at the Hard Rock Café in Boston, and I said, "Yes" to dinner.

On our 6 hour dinner date, we told each other our stories. I'm sure he was thinking that I had an enormous amount of baggage, and I certainly thought, "Well, this guy is totally screwed up!" As I listened to his story, though, I realized we had more in common than I originally thought. By the end of our date, I found myself hoping we would see each other again—we had a lot to talk about! Yes, we did go on another date, and we have now been talking for 20 years; first as a couple, then as business partners, then husband and wife, and finally as parents.

After one year of dating, Jonathan left on tour with a non-profit speakers program talking to kids about drug addiction. I closed the club at the end of the comedy boom and went on tour with Jesus Christ Superstar. As we rolled past the interminable cornfields that bus tours must suffer, Carl Anderson (the original Judas) told me daily that I should take what I knew and start my own lecture series with Jonathan. As the tour was ending, I approached Jonathan with the idea. In typical addict fashion, he was

179

convinced it would never work, but as you can see, my wisdom prevailed!

6.3 Miles To Go Begins: Miles To Go started in earnest on Jonathan's 41st birthday. Kelly was growing weary of the lifestyle of the Broadway bus tour—put on the show, pack it up, drive all night, then wake up in yet another parking lot at another faceless venue. Jonathan was worn down by the demands of being a travelling drug educator--the constant air travel and the not-so-subtle dysfunctional dynamics of 22 recovering-addict educators trying to determine a pecking order. Kelly, always the visionary, had a plan. She was convinced we could take Jonathan's sense of humor, combine it with the story of his addiction and her role as caregiver and fixer of addicts, and with her knowledge of business and dramatic presentation create a better way to do drug education. We spent the next year developing a lecture series about addiction and drugs that was fun, scientific, and medically accurate while simultaneously retaining the power and emotion of our life stories.

We wanted our program to go beyond the slogan-based drug education so popular in that era. For too long, kids had been responding to drug education with rolling eyes and arms crossed over their chests—we wanted to educate, entertain, and engage them. Finally, in September of 1996, with the fundamentals of our program firmly in place, we moved back to California and started teaching. Our program became popular faster than we ever imagined, and we've been at it ever since. We are now, officially, "The drug guys."

References and Links:

Our website: www.milestogodrugeducation.com -- All of our handbooks are available on our website.

Books and Websites:
Association for Psychological Science (2008, September 11). Why Delaying Gratification Is Smart#.TmuUdhjZpiM.email. *ScienceDaily*. Retrieved September 25, 2011, from http://www.sciencedaily.com /releases/2008/09/080909111022.htm#.TmuUdhjZpiM.email

Ballantine Books. More about Dr. Tannen's work at: http://www9.georgetown.edu/faculty/tannend/bio.html

California Department of Alcoholic Beverage Control. http://www.abc.ca.gov/teencorner.html

McGraw, Jay. (2000) *Life Strategies For Teens*. Clearwater, Florida. Touchtone Books.

Merriam-Webster 2011. http://www.merriam-webster.com/

Moorman, Chick. (1998) *Parent Talk: How to Talk to Your Children in Language That Builds Self-Esteem and Encourages Responsibility*. New York: Fireside Books. More about Chick Moorman: http://chickmoorman.com/

Tannen, Deborah. (1990). *You Just Don't Understand, Women and Men in Conversation*. New York:

Weill Cornell Medical College (2011, September 1). Marshmallow test points to biological basis for delayed gratification#.Tl-WnSJuzfk.email. *ScienceDaily*. Retrieved September 25, 2011, from http://www.sciencedaily.com

Brain Development: This section is based on information we have shared in our lecture series over the last 18 years. The following links will lead you to some highly informative sites that will allow you to explore the fascinating topic of teen brain development:
http://science.education.nih.gov/Customers.nsf/HSBrain?OpenForm ;
http://www.nimh.nih.gov/health/publications/the-teen-brain-still-under-construction/complete-index.shtml ; http://www.livestrong.com/article/525409-what-are-two-physical-changes-that-take-place-in-the-teen-brain/?utm_source=popslideshow&utm_medium=al ;
http://www.livestrong.com/article/493513-teen-brain-development/ ;
http://www.pbs.org/wgbh/pages/frontline/shows/teenbrain/work/adolescent.html ;
http://teenbrain.drugfree.org/science/index.html

Alcohol Specific:
"Fact Sheets, Underage Drinking". CDC. July 20, 2010. August 23, 2010
http://www.cdc.gov/alcohol/fact-sheets/underage-drinking.htm

Alcohol plays a role: . http://www.ehow.com/info_7926461_alcohol-teenagers.html ;

Almost 75% of teen drinkers: http://www.caraccidentadvice.com/statisticsofteendrunkdriving.html

New studies from 2011: University of Cincinnati. "Possible brain damage in young adult binge-drinkers revealed in new study." *ScienceDaily*, 27 Jun. 2011. Web. 28 Jun. 2011.

Occasional heavy drinking: Teen Drinking May Cause Irreversible Brain Damage
http://www.npr.org/templates/story/story.php?storyId=122765890 ;

Teens that binge drink: Continuity of Binge and Harmful Drinking From Late Adolescence to Early Adulthood http://pediatrics.aappublications.org/content/114/3/714.abstract ;

181

Peer Pressure:
Evidence exists that says children do not necessarily: Peer Pressure ...An Often Misunderstood concept http://www.extension.umn.edu/distribution/familydevelopment/00092.html

In other words, it is not so much: Teens and Peer Pressure http://www.webmd.com/parenting/teen abuse-cough-medicine-9/peer-pressure

One aspect of peer pressure parents: THE EFFECTS OF PEER PRESSURE ON TEENAGERS HTTP://WWW.LIVESTRONG.COM/ARTICLE/511686-THE-EFFECTS-OF-PEER-PRESSURE-ON-TEENAGERS/

One of the most powerful protective: How to Cope With Peer Pressure http://www.wikihow.com/Cope-With-Peer-Pressure

European Data:
"Children 'risking liver disease'". BBC NEWS. November 22, 2008. August 23, 2010 http://news.bbc.co.uk/2/hi/uk_news/7743265.stm

"Drink Like the French, Die Like the French". Marin Institute. August 4, 2008. August 22, 2010 http://www.marininstitute.org/site/big-alcohol/15-industry-tactics/111-the-french-paradox-health-and-alcohol-use-in-france.html?start=8

Guerrini, I. "Alcohol Consumption and Heavy Drinking: A Survey in Three Italian Villages". Alcohol and Alcoholism. February 14, 2006. August 23, 2010 http://alcalc.oxfordjournals.org/cgi/content/full/41/3/336

"Youth Drinking Rates and Problems: A Comparison of European Countries and the United States". Join Together. 2005. August 23, 2010 http://www.jointogether.org/resources/youth-drinking-rates-and-a-of.html

Substance Abuse:
Dalton Ph.D., Madeline. "Relation between Parental Restrictions on Movies and Adolescent Use of Tobacco and Alcohol". ACP American College of Physicians. January/February 2002. August 23, 2010 http://www.acponline.org/clinical_information/journals_publications/ecp/janfeb02/dalton.htm

"Drug Abuse and Addiction". NIDA. July 28, 2010. August 23, 2010 http://drugabuse.gov/scienceofaddiction/addiction.html

Emery, Chris. "Youthful Media Exposure Holds Promise and Peril". Medpage TODAY. March 1, 2010. August 23, 2010 http://www.medpagetoday.com/Pediatrics/Parenting/18735

"Drug Abuse and Addiction". NIDA. July 28, 2010. August 23, 2010 http://drugabuse.gov/scienceofaddiction/addiction.html

"Factors of Teen Drug Use". Adolescent Substance Abuse Knowledge Base. 2007. August 23, 2010 http://www.adolescent-substance-abuse.com/

Family:
Gilman, SE, et al. "Parental smoking and adolescent smoking initiation: and intergenerational perspective on tobacco control". PubMed.gov. February, 2009. August 23, 2010 http://www.ncbi.nlm.nih.gov/pubmed/19171580

"Families, Friends, Schools and Neighborhoods Contribute to Adolescent Alcohol Misuse". Science Daily. November 17, 2008. August 23, 2010 http://www.sciencedaily.com/releases/2008/11/081114080917.htm

"Parents Pivotal in Keeping Teens Away From Drugs, Reveals New Data". PARENTS. THE ANTI-DRUG. February 9, 2006. August 23, 2010 http://www.theantidrug.com/news/press-release.aspx?id=19

"The Importance of Family Dinners V". The National Center on Addiction and Substance Abuse at Columbia University (CASA). September 23, 2009. August 23, 2010 http://www.casacolumbia.org/templates/PressReleases.aspx?articleid=567&zoneid=66

"Key Findings of the 2008 Partnership Attitude Tracking Study on Teen Drug Abuse". The Partnership for a Drug-Free America. May 1, 2009. August 23, 2010 http://www.drugfree.org/Portal/2008_Partnership_Attitude_Tracking_Study

Prescription Abuse:
"Misuse of Prescription Drugs Common Among H.S. Students". Join Together. June 7, 2010. August 23, 2010 http://www.jointogether.org/news/research/summaries/2010/misuse-of-prescription-drugs.html

"Prescription Drug Abuse". MedlinePlus. March 22, 2010. August 23, 2010 http://www.nlm.nih.gov/medlineplus/prescriptiondrugabuse.html

"Prescription Painkillers Becoming More Popular than Marijuana, SAMHSA Says". Join Together. October 30, 2006. August 23, 2010 http://www.jointogether.org/news/research/summaries/2006/prescription-painkillers.html

Not All Kids Do Drugs For Teens
Lessons In Drug Prevention: Handbook Four
Proactive Techniques For Teens

To order any of our products or services, please visit:
www.milestogodrugeducation.com
Kelly Townsend, Psy.D. & Jonathan Scott

183

54415625R00107

Made in the USA
San Bernardino, CA
16 October 2017